Passage to Destiny

Dedicated to the memory of my best friend, my father,
and all the men and women who lost their lives on
Saturday, 12th February 1944.

1. Percival Crabb (Buster) 1915–91 photographed in his Chief Petty
Officer's uniform in 1944.

PASSAGE TO DESTINY

THE SINKING OF THE
S.S. KHEDIVE ISMAIL
IN THE SEA WAR
AGAINST JAPAN

BRIAN JAMES CRABB

PAUL WATKINS
STAMFORD
1 9 9 7

Typeset and designed
using the discs of the author
by the publisher

PAUL WATKINS
18 Adelaide Street
Stamford
Lincolnshire, PE9 2EN

ISBN

1 900289 10 5

Printed and bound by Woolnoughs of Irthlingborough

CONTENTS

ACKNOWLEDGEMENTS

In the January 1977 issue of *Navy News* there was a brief and inaccurate mention of the sinking of the SS *Khedive Ismail* in February 1944. My father, Percival Crabb, immediately responded to this article, telling his family that the ship sank on a Saturday, not a Sunday as reported. We knew very few details and encouraged him to write his own account and send it to the editor, though not before we all had photocopies. After my father's unexpected death in December 1991, I resolved to find out as much as I could about the incident. Research soon established not only that there was very little published information on the tragedy, but that these few accounts were riddled with errors, despite the fact that the sinking of the *Khedive Ismail* was the third worst merchant shipping disaster in the history of the Second World War.

The cover picture has been painted by the reputable marine artist Robert Blackwell and depicts the *Khedive Ismail* being struck by the second torpedo. Only he could create such a fascinating and dramatic scene on canvas. I am truly indebted to him, especially for keeping to such a tight schedule. I would also like to thank Jim Crissup for his expert advice on the flags displayed in the painting.

Several survivors helped me visualise the incident. Gloria Smith (*née* West) sent me a copy of the diary she had kept of her experiences of the preceeding events and the actual sinking; she also answered many of my varied questions. Dan Docwra, Bill Howard, Tom Fox and Eddie Turner each gave their time to correspond and be personally interviewed. Their stories, all different, are truly remarkable. Sadly, Dan and Bill died in December 1994 and 1995, respectively and I am truly sad that they never saw the finished narrative.

Thanks are also due to two independent eye-witnesses: Cliff Horrell had been a gunner on board the SS *Varsova*. I tracked him down by searching numerous telephone directories. His account, along with that by Ted Barber (who was recently tracked down by Cliff: they met in Torquay in June 1996 after 52 years. Ted died the following September), is probably the most accurate concerning the actual sinking, as they were positioned on the stern of their troopship, attending to one of the guns, and were undoubtedly the first to spot the submarine's periscope. They were able to see the starboard side of the stricken troopship and observe the whole process of her final destruction. Cliff was also helpful in sharing his detailed memories of the Board of Enquiry.

I would also like to express my gratitude to Patrick Breen (son of the late Patrick Breen) and Maureen Macaire (related to Roy Henbest), for their permission to include sensitive material concerning the disaster. Sheila Hamnett (who, along with Shelagh Robinson, organised a memorial service at the Wrens' church at St Mary le Strand, London, fifty years after the sinking) has been extremely helpful in sending me copies of accounts along with putting me in touch with some of the survivors and relatives.

Whilst on holiday in Malta, I was fortunate enough to trace Michael Cassar, a well known author and collector of maritime photographs. I am grateful to him for supplying, and allowing me to use, some interesting pictures of the *Khedive Ismail* and an advertisement from a 1939 Maltese newspaper.

David Miller, author and researcher, has also been a great help in lending material and the photographs he had discovered when he was considering writing about the same subject; he also revealed other sources of information concerning the Army. Thanks are also due to Gus Britton, a researcher at the Submarine Museum at Gosport, for, amongst other things, sending me interesting facts about the Japanese submarine *I-27* .

Others, who have all contributed in an equal manner, include survivors A. Walker RN, Lieutenant-Colonel J. A. Stevens, OBE and the late Phyllis Hutchinson for their accounts of the sinking of the troopship. Reg Crang RN, Douglas Freer RN and Jack Hall RN (HMS *Petard*), Bill Hiscock RN and Lawrence Horn RN (HMS *Hawkins*) also gave me their observations of the incident. I would also like to thank Gilbert Wan MN who worked on troopships throughout the War and graphically described his catering experiences and aspects of life aboard one.

Regarding the history of the SS *Aconcagua*, I would like to thank Maria Ines Herrera, from the Public Relations Department of CSAV Sud Americana de Vapores, Valparaiso, Chile and Alfonso Garcia, proprietor of the Black Horse at Clapton-in-Gordano, who painstakingly translated the Spanish information supplied.

Members of various institutions have also helped: the librarians of the Public Records Office at Kew, Surrey; Miss J. M. Wraight, National Maritime Museum; Mrs Eileen Edwards, archives assistant, Merseyside Maritime Museum; Miss Vanna Skelley, manager, Business Record Centre, University of Glasgow; Declan Barriskill, principal reference librarian, and Valerie Hart, at the Guildhall Library, London; Janice Davis, p.p. historical secretary, Royal Artillery Historical Trust, Woolwich; and the librarians at Birmingham, Bristol and Plymouth. In the search for some photographs of three of British India Line's ships that were in convoy KR8, I would like to thank Lyn Palmer who is an Information Officer at P&O, London. Lastly, I am indebted to Christian Woodhouse for his substantial help in one specific area of research, concerning the numbers of naval personnel on board the ship.

Some of the photographs were lacking in contrast; this substantial problem was kindly rectified by my brother, Rodney Crabb. I would also like to thank my cousin David Hunt who found time to look up information from various Lloyd's publications. The late Gordon Connell (author of *Fighting Destroyer*), his wife Joan and son Michael also deserve a special mention for providing several survivors' accounts. Another unsung hero is my good friend Richard Skuse who has made many constructive suggestions in due course.

Linda Hills, Jill Truman and Rita Nichols also deserve a special mention for their help on various aspects of the manuscript and research material.

Last but not least, I would like to thank my wife Angela and my two daughters, Anna and Helen, who believed and supported me throughout the 4½ years which the book has taken to write and research.

If I have unwittingly omitted anyone who has contributed towards the final text, I trust that the oversight will be forgiven. Although I have thoroughly researched the story of the incident, I am always interested in any constructive criticism or further information, via the publisher.

Brian J. Crabb

INTRODUCTION

In the most authoritative history of the naval war against the Japanese, the historian Arthur J. Marder mentioned the *Khedive Ismail* incident in the following brief sentence:

> A thousand WRNS, nurses, and Auxiliary Territorial Service (ATS) girls lost their lives with the *Khedive Ismail*, which sank within two minutes, one of the few troopships sunk during the entire war and sunk by a Japanese boat that had courageously penetrated the convoy's escort screen. [*Old Friends, New Enemies. The Royal Navy and the Imperial Japanese Navy*, volume 2: *The Pacific War, 1942–1945* (Oxford: Clarendon Press, 1990), p. 254.]

Apart from the extraordinary errors of fact in this statement, the significance of the incident as the third largest merchant shipping disaster in the history of the war, and the worst disaster involving the loss of women, is not highlighted. The *Khedive Ismail* incident is largely ignored by naval historians, and the only previous accounts of the incident, by G. G. Connell, in *Fighting Destroyer. The Story of HMS Petard* (London: William Kimber, 1976) and two 1990 issues of *Warship World*, are not only short and uninformative, but also contain many errors.

The misinformation about the incident extends even to Winston Churchill's account of the war. He reports in *The Second World War*, Volume V, that he made the following enquiry on 19th March 1944:

> *Prime Minister to First Lord and First Sea Lord*
> This is a serious disaster. Who were the 1,055 drowned? Were they troops outward or homeward bound? British or American? How is it that in a convoy of this kind more could not be rescued?*

The printed footnote reads:

> *The British transport *Khedive Ismail*, proceeding in convoy from East Africa to Ceylon, was torpedoed by a Japanese U-boat near Addu Atoll on February 12th, and sank in two minutes. She carried 1,947 passengers, including British, American, and African troops and members of the Women's Services. The U-boat was sunk soon afterwards by British destroyers.

1

But Churchill was incorrect. No Americans were on board and the inflated figure of 1,947 is 436 too many.

The story that you are about to read is entirely factual and uncovers the true account of the tragic loss of the troopship *Khedive Ismail*. My own interest stems from my late father's fortunate survival. When I began my research I only knew my father's account, the day it sank and the chapter in Gordon Connell's book. Since then, my extensive research has taken me to the Public Records Office and the Guildhall Library in London and the central libraries of Birmingham, Bristol and Plymouth. I have travelled many miles to interview the few people who still survive who were actually involved in the incident. All the survivors and eye-witnesses I interviewed were generous with their time. Sadly, their numbers are dwindling but none of them will ever forget the sudden attack that took place on that sunny and peaceful Saturday afternoon.

As I became more involved with the story, and started to accumulate material, I became determined to unearth the records of the Board of Enquiry, should they survive. On their eventual discovery I found the complete list of survivors and it was only then that I decided, if it was possible, that I would try to find the names of all those who lost their lives as well and preserve them in book form.

The Board of Enquiry was not easy to find. It was not listed under 'Board of Enquiry' as most other reports on ship sinkings are. I eventually found it under files headed 'Reports of enemy submarine attacks on merchant shipping'. The report was there, together with the list of survivors taken on board HMS *Petard*, including the misspelled name of my father. It is almost certainly the case that sensitivity over the event had resulted in a forty-year hold being placed upon this file, hence the difficulty in locating it today.

Researching the complete list of those who lost their lives was a mammoth task which took several years to complete and was only achieved by sifting through all the Memorial Registers published by the War Graves Commission (with a little help from one source which I cannot mention for fear of jeopardising his or her job). In many cases the date of death was the only clue to their being involved in the incident. The effort was worth it and the list here printed is a memorial to those who lost their lives on that fateful day.

The significance of the incident, however, is not simply because it was a considerable human tragedy. The story reveals much about the conduct of war at the time and the strategic thinking of both the allies and the Japanese.

I

THE EARLY HISTORY OF SS
ACONCAGUA/KHEDIVE ISMAIL

The passenger liner whose fate was to be the third worst merchant shipping disaster throughout the Second World War was originally built for the Compania Sud Americana de Vapores of Chile in 1920–2 by the Scott Shipbuilding and Engineering Company Limited at Greenock, Scotland and launched, on 11th February 1922, by Olga Budge de Edwards, wife of the Chilean Ambassador in London. She was named SS *Aconcagua*, after one of the rivers of Chile (a tradition still carried out by the same company today). She was much larger than any previous ships owned by the company and was specifically designed and built for an expanding and relatively new trade with the east coast of North America.

She was 422 feet long, 56 feet wide, with a draught of 30 feet, and her gross tonnage was 7,513 tons. She was designed for carrying both cargo and 243 passengers (155 First Class and 88 Third Class). The cost of her construction was £575,000, a price somewhat higher than the original estimate, the increase being due to modifications to the original plans ordered by the owners, which included the decision to convert her from coal-burning to oil-fuel.

Her machinery consisted of two high/low pressure steam turbines developing 1,469 horse power which was transmitted through single reduction gearboxes to twin screw shafts. Power was obtained from six, single-ended, corrugated boilers working at 215 lb pressure, which had also been built by Scott's of Greenock. To her builders she was ship No. 516 and her subsequent entry into the Lloyd's register recorded her official number as 1132 (call sign HBLP). There was also a sister ship, called *Teno*, which was completed some months later for the same South American customer and built by the same shipbuilding company.

During her acceptance trials she achieved a creditable speed of 17½ knots and left London on 10th August 1922. Her first Captain, John Carswell, was the British commodore of the Chilean shipping company.

2. SS *Aconcagua*, in about the mid 1920s.

3. Stern view of the *Aconcagua*, again in the mid 1920s.

She arrived at Valparaiso (where she was registered) on 18th September and entered straight into service. Between 1922 and late 1929 she plied exclusively from the ports of Chile, through the newly opened Panama Canal, to Brooklyn, New York. A typical run would see her loading at Valparaiso then sailing northwards, calling at Arica, Mollendo and Callao, before negotiating the various locks at Miraflores and Pedro Miguel. Once through these, she would pass through the narrow jungle-sided canal before crossing Gatun Lake and the complex of locks at Gatun. The whole area was, and still is, known as the Panama Canal Zone. Brief stops were sometimes incurred at either Cristobal or Colon, on the Pacific side, or Balboa on the Atlantic side, before heading northward to the 'Big Apple'. After discharging, she re-loaded and retraced the voyage. The round trip usually took about eight weeks to complete, a journey bisected by her sister ship *Teno*, to maintain a regular and scheduled service.

Her first entry into the Lloyd's weekly Casualty Reports occurred on 18th February 1924, when it was reported that her forward section had touched the sea bed whilst leaving the port of San Antonio, about fifty miles south of Valparaiso. However, a subsequent report, recorded some weeks later, denied the account as erroneous.

On 30th December 1926 the *Aconcagua* ran aground in 4 fathoms of water off La Libertad, at Salinas in Equador; she was en route from Valparaiso to New York. She was refloated the following evening after jettisoning some of her cargo of nitrate. Divers inspected her at Cristobal on 30th January 1927 and she was eventually surveyed at a New York dry dock after discharging her cargo. There was no apparent damage.

In April 1928, whilst still trading with the same ports, she was administered by W. Hamilton & Co. Eventually, due to internal company problems, she was subsequently managed by Lowden, Connell & Co. Ltd., of Liverpool.

On the day of her arrival from Arica, 23rd May 1928, the *Aconcagua* anchored and moored to a buoy at Corral (south of Valparaiso) awaiting a berth. During extremely bad weather she came into contact with the 3,171 ton, British owned, ship called *Karnak* (owned by Moss Steamship Co. Ltd.) which sustained damage above the waterline.

On 13th September 1928, whilst berthed at Pier 29, Brooklyn, the Chilean steamer caught fire in No. 5 hold. Although the fire was eventually extinguished the next day by the local fire department, their task was assisted by local tugs which tied up alongside and provided extra water and appliances. The laden cargo was appreciably damaged by both fire and water. Subsequent salvage operations must have commenced almost immediately as the steamer was only delayed for four or five days.

With her last mishap still fresh in the minds of all concerned it was hardly surprising if the next calamity caused some blushes when, leaving her berth at the Aduana Mole in Valparaiso, the *Aconcagua* fouled the moorings of a target raft belonging to the Chilean Navy. In turn this caused the raft to swing round and strike No. 10 hopper, cutting a plate at the water-line and springing several rivets, causing a leak.

On 24th June 1931 she was immobilised at Valparaiso and eventually handed over to Lithgows Ltd., on 6th August 1932, at Callao in Peru, as part of a two-ship deal involving the sistership *Teno,* thus alleviating a substantial debt owed to her new owners by Compania Sud Americana de Vapores. It caused a national outcry, when Chilean newspapers revealed that the deal had been carried out without the consent of the Company's shareholders.

The *Aconcagua* (along with the *Teno*) was put up for sale. From 14th December 1932 the two ships were laid up at the Kyles of Bute until late 1934, initially at Kames Bay but, at a later date, they were moved north-eastward to the more sheltered anchorage of Tighnabruich (both ports being north-west of the Isle of Bute, Scotland, and conveniently near the main shipping route of the River and Firth of Clyde). Her agents, Messrs. Robert Duncan and Co., organised skeleton crews and security procedures whilst prospective buyers were invited to inspect the dormant vessels.

It was on 18th January 1934, that a raging storm hit the shores of the Scottish Isles, causing the mothballed *Aconcagua,* and her sister ship, to drag their anchors whilst off the shores of Tighnabruich. Tugs were dispatched from Greenock to stand by and assist. Similar incidents occurred all around the western shores of Britain until the storm finally blew itself out. The same year, and place, saw more excitement when, on October 29th, an oil-fuel explosion took place on the *Aconcagua* whilst preliminary starting procedures were being carried out. Although there was no structural damage to the vessel, two of the ship's firemen were seriously burned, about the head and neck. An undetected accumulation of old gas was the suggested, and probable, cause.

During March 1935 the two liners were sold for £75,000 each (£500,000 less than the price charged her first owners) to the Khedivial Mail Steamship & Graving Dock Company Limited of Alexandria, Egypt. The *Aconcagua* was renamed *Khedive Ismail.* She was reregistered in London (whilst her sister ship was reregistered in Alexandria), and sailed from

4. SS *Khedive Ismail* steaming out of the River Clyde, 17th April 1935.

Greenock on 17th April the same year, and arrived at Gibraltar on 9th May (her new official Lloyd's number became 162372 and her call sign MKGG).

Using Alexandria as her base port, she now began a Mediterranean trade between Alexandria and Marseilles, calling at Piraeus, Naples and Genoa. Her captains thoughout the forthcoming period included E. Eliot, J. P. Thomson and J. T. Harvey, and her new role was complemented, once more, by her sister ship *Teno*, which was renamed *Mohamed Ali El-Kebir*. The combined use of these two liners introduced a regular passenger service, meeting a recent increase in demand. As in Chile, the two ships carried both passengers and general cargoes on these journeys.

Khedive Ismail's new name commemorated the former ruler of Egypt, during the period of Turkish occupation of the country, who was the father of the contemporary king, Fuad I (who died in 1936). Ismail had been the second son of Ibrahim Pasha (Pasha meaning governor); he was born in 1830 and became Ismail Pasha in 1863 and Khedive (viceroy) in 1867. His

8

5. Side profile showing off her pleasing shape, 17th April 1935.

reign was a period of large public investment and economic expansion, especially in cotton cultivation, but unfortunately his financial borrowings led to bankruptcy in 1875, followed by an imposition of European financial control and an encroachment on his political authority. When Ismail attempted to resist the process he was deposed in 1879 by the Ottoman government, following Anglo-French representations. He died in 1895 whilst Turkish rule continued until 1914. His family survived the crisis, however, and continued to rule until King Farouk was deposed by General Nasser in the 1950s.

In 1936, Haifa was added to the list of commerce (although this additional port was only traded with for that year). However, the successive years, from 1937 to 1940, saw the addition of Malta to the busy schedule of both ships. Passengers could depart from the island in either direction each month. On 29th August 1938 the *Khedive Ismail* collided with, and sank, a fishing vessel off the coast of Malta but, as no record of the event

6. SS *Khedive Ismail* entering the Grand Harbour, Malta, 31st March 1939, on one of her scheduled runs from Alexandria. Her funnel was painted bottle-green with a black top.

appears in Lloyd's Weekly Casualty Reports for this period, it appears that there were no fatalities.

On the 7th October 1938, an extraordinary general meeting was held at the London offices of the 40-year-old Khedivial Mail Steamship and Graving Dock Company. It was announced that an agreement had been signed for the transfer of all assets, including seven steamships, to the Pharaonic Mail Line S.A.E. of Cairo and Alexandria, Egypt. The sale did not entirely liquidate the company, however. The newly formed Khedivial Mail Agency, Ltd, became the shipping agents for the new owners and retained a small headquarters in London.

With stability rapidly changing in the Mediterranean area due to the expected declaration of war, against the Allies by the Italians (which took place on 10th June 1940), the Pharaonic Mail Line decided to take a precautionary measure. On 10th May 1940, the *Khedive Ismail* sailed from Alexandria on a new trade route, still incorporating cargo/passenger facilities, but not on a scheduled service – instead she traded around the

7. Another view, taken on the same afternoon, showing the liner just inside the
Grand Harbour entrance.

East African ports and the various routes offered there. Her southerly
voyage took her through the Suez Canal to Aden whereupon she set course
for Kilindini (the port for Mombasa), in Kenya, East Africa. She then sailed
eastward to the small port of Tamatave, in Madagascar, where she arrived at
the end of May. In the early part of June the steamer entered the port of
Durban in South Africa before continuing south-west to Cape Town.
However, on the 14th June whilst sailing back to Durban, she encountered
a violent storm which caused heavy weather damage and washed one of her
lifeboats overboard. She returned to Cape Town for repairs, detaining her
departure for one week.

Meanwhile, her sister ship, the *Mohamed Ali El-Kebir*, had been
requisitioned for war work just after the outbreak of war. After arriving
from Liverpool she had sailed from Avonmouth during the morning of
August 5th 1940 and was carrying 860 troops and naval personnel. She was
bound for Gibraltar and was sailing independently with one destroyer as
her escort; and carrying out No. 15 zig-zag pattern at 15 knots. On August

11

8. Her sister ship, SS *Mohamed Ali El-Kebir,* berthed stern-first between SS *Arandora Star*
and the Italian SS *Città di Trieste,* beside the St Barbara Bastion, Malta
(none of these ships survived the War).

7th, at 20.42, west of Northern Ireland (in position 55° 08´N 13° 18´W), she was
torpedoed by a German U-boat on the starboard quarter, very near the
stern. She took two hours to sink and 740 Royal Navy, Army and ship's
personnel were rescued.

On October 6th 1940, whilst the *Khedive Ismail* was in Bombay, the ship
was requisitioned by the Ministry of War Transport for use as a troopship.
She sailed to Mombasa and arrived at Table Bay on 21st October and for
the remainder of the month she underwent the necessary modifications
required by her new owners. As with most merchant ships commandeered
for war work, conversion included the addition of some armament.
Typically, she was equipped with one 4-inch and one 12 lb gun aft, with six
oerlikons spaced at strategic positions around the vessel, which were
manned by both Royal Navy personnel and soldiers of the Maritime Regiment. Her colours were changed from her pre-war company livery to
light-grey from the waterline upwards, whilst the hull was painted black,

REGULAR DE-LUXE EXPRESS PASSENGER AND CARGO SERVICE

ALEXANDRIA - MALTA - MARSEILLES AND VICE VERSA

By T.S.S. *Khedive Ismail & Mohamed Ali El-Kebir* 12,000 tons.

FOR MARSEILLES		FOR ALEXANDRIA	
NOVEMBER	13th	DECEMBER	3rd & 30th
DECEMBER	11th	JANUARY	27th
JANUARY	8th	FEBRUARY	25th
FEBRUARY	5th	MARCH	24th
MARCH	5th	APRIL	21st
APRIL	2nd & 30th.		

For further information apply to the Agents:—

BIANCHI & CO. (MALTA) LTD.

30D, Strada Zaccaria, Valletta.—*Tel. 620 & 671.*

9. Advertisement displayed in 1939 in one of Malta's
daily newspapers, showing the schedule of both ships.

similar to the colour scheme used by most Royal Naval ships operating in these warmer climes.

On April 24th 1941 she sailed from Alexandria and experienced her first war action, taking part in the evacuation from Návplion, south-west of Athens; with a full complement of Army personnel, she proceeded to Suda Bay, in Crete, where she arrived on the 27th. (She had transported a small part of the 45,000 Greek, British and Commonwealth soldiers that were eventually rescued from the mainland before the capitulation of Crete, when it was successfully invaded by German airborne forces on the morning of May 20th.) *Khedive Ismail's* dangerous voyage also saw her first experience of gunfire, from aircraft of the Luftwaffe. Her mission was favourably completed when she reached Alexandria on the 29th April.

However, it was not until August 2nd 1941 that the Lloyd's List and Shipping Gazette reported that a Lloyd's survey had been held on May 5th at Suez Roads. It revealed several small holes in her shell plating, on the starboard bow, and many perforations of varying sizes in the fore mast, crow's nest, forward and lower bridge bulkhead plating and funnel. Some stays, supporting the rigging, were severed whilst there was also some damage to the officers' and other cabins. The degaussing cable insulation was also damaged. Repairs were effected immediately when she was made seaworthy at Suez, by the 25th May, and she sailed for Bombay (via Aden) arriving on 18th June.

For the rest of her working life she was explicitly used in the Indian Ocean, the Red Sea and Persian Gulf areas for the movement of troops to and from India and East Africa (initially reinforcing the North African campaign, and later moving troops from Africa to Colombo ready for the offensive against the Japanese). Her movements were managed by British India Steam Navigation Company Limited, who were familiar with the trading routes of the Far East. In the ensuing years her list of ports included: Suez, Port Said, Port Sudan, Djibouti, Aden, Abadan (for refuelling stops), Karachi, Bombay, Colombo, Tamatave, Mombasa, Tanga, Durban, Port Elizabeth, Table Bay and Diego Suarez; although not in that order and depending on the requisite movements desired by the War Office at any given time. The earliest date discovered, from PRO records, for this period, is the 9th July 1942, when she sailed from Kilindini escorted by HMS *Arrow*. She joined convoy CM29 at noon on the 11th, about 200 miles due east of Mombasa. She was carrying troop reinforcements for the final push in North Africa and delivered her valuable cargo to Suez on 26th July after a nine-day stop in Aden.

After an extensive three-month survey in Port Elizabeth, South Africa, which was completed on March 10th 1943, her existing Passenger Carrying Certificate was endorsed and extended, and she was immediately put back into active service. She sailed in a nine-ship convoy, CM40, which departed from Durban on 22nd March 1943. The convoy reached Kilindini on the 31st of the same month, before continuing on to Suez which she reached in the middle of April. She arrived at Durban on the 19th May and, on 27th May, whilst at Port Natal, during discharging operations, she sustained damage to No. 11 lifeboat, caused by a brush with the wharf rather than enemy action. She had another accident whilst in dry-dock (at Port Natal), when a fire broke out in No. 1 lower hold on 17th June. Access could only be made by gas-cutting two starboard shell plates. Three lower 'tween deck plates and two hatch beams were buckled whilst twenty stringers, a store compartment and a division bulkhead, all wooden, were burnt, but such was the demand for troopships, at that time, that essential repairs were effected immediately whilst other repairs were dealt with at a later date, convenient to her captain and the Ministry of War Transport.

Captain R. W. M. Whiteman DSC joined the ship, for the first time, on 18th June (the day after the fire). Although this was the first time he had sailed on the *Khedive Ismail* he had captained the *Mohamed Ali El Kebir*, for a period, from 2nd June 1937. However, it was not until 27th July that the *Khedive Ismail* was back at sea in a small two-ship convoy escorted by HMS *Alaunia*. Convoy KA8 included the steamship *Salween* and reached Aden on schedule, and without incident, on the 2nd August. Returning to East Africa she sailed from Kilindini, on 24th August, in convoy KR6. The three-ship convoy, including the troopships *Nevasa* and *Nieuw Holland*, progressed eastwards to a position just north of the Seychelles with local escort. It was then taken over by the destroyer HMS *Racehorse*, the only A/S escort available for the last part of the passage. The voyage was completed successfully on 4th September, when it arrived at Colombo.

Captain Whiteman was selected as commodore of a seven-ship convoy, BA50, which sailed from Bombay on 12th October 1943, arrived at Aden on the 20th and concluded at Suez on the 25th. Interestingly enough, no zig-zag was performed on this journey. On 2nd November 1943, the *Khedive Ismail* sailed from Aden in a 34-ship two-section convoy (AP51/AB19) with two escorts for each group; their destinations were Bombay and Colombo. On 5th November, 17 ships departed eastwards to Bombay whilst the others, including the *Khedive Ismail*, steamed on southwards with local A/S escort being provided by the destroyer HMS *Quickmatch*. It also reached a satisfactory conclusion on the 8th, when the remaining part of the convoy was safely delivered.

During the middle of January the large troopship *Strathaird*, which had sailed from Liverpool (via the Suez Canal and the Red Sea), had arrived at Kilindini. She had disembarked nearly half of her original Army and Navy consignment before shipping the remaining personnel to Durban. With no suitable accommodation readily available in and around the city of Mombasa, most of the junior ranks were billeted under canvas, inland from the port, some being earmarked for transportation in a forthcoming convoy.

Many troop movements were taking place in the December/January period, and further use of the *Khedive Ismail* was inevitable. She had just completed a westbound convoy on 28th January from Colombo (via Dar-es-Salaam and Zanzibar) to Kilindini, in the company of the troopships *Varsova*, *Ekma* and *Ellenga*. Reinforcements were needed for the attempt to retake Burma and these four ships, along with the *City of Paris*, which had arrived from Bombay on 1st February, were chosen to be the nucleus of a very important convoy, codenamed KR8. The valuable troop-carrying exercise was scheduled to sail from Mombasa during the early part of February 1944 and its arrival was eagerly awaited at Colombo.

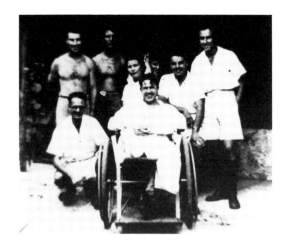

10. Buster (in the wheelchair) recovering from a broken leg at the
87th General Hospital, Nairobi.

11. Buster dressed and ready to join the SS *Khedive Ismail*, February 3rd 1944.

II

CONVOY KR8

Percival Crabb, nicknamed Buster as soon as he joined the Navy, was awakened during the early hours of Thursday, 3rd February 1944 and began to prepare himself for the long journey ahead. He had been recovering at the 87th General Hospital, in Nairobi, for just over six months from a broken leg received during a football match while he had been serving on HMS *Kenya*. His right leg was still in plaster which made it somewhat awkward for him to dress in his petty officer's uniform, an attire he had not worn since July the previous year. After a good lunch he was picked up and driven to the railway station in the centre of the capital. The station was thronging with the arrival of a large contingent of nursing sisters and army personnel obviously waiting for the same excursion. After several hours the train departed during the early evening for Mombasa; meanwhile, everyone settled down for the night-time journey, descending from the high plateau towards their destination. As night grew into day the passengers were soon appreciating the breathtaking views of the African landscape and by early morning the train was entering the bustling city of Mombasa. The special excursion continued on through the city to the dockside area of Kilindini.

During the long journey Buster had reflected on his relaxed recovery at the hospital. When he had arrived from HMS *Kenya* he had been taken for X-rays, which revealed that the tibia was displaced and would need resetting. This would involve re-breaking the leg before the misaligned shin bone could be properly straightened. The following day he was wheeled into an operating theatre, stripped from the waist down and cleaned up prior to having his right leg reset.

The hospital was situated in pleasant surroundings with palm trees and other exotic plants dotted about in acres of ground. The nursing staff and the Swahili cleaners were full of fun and, during the lazy afternoons, they had spent many hilarious hours telling yarns or playing games under a long grass-covered lean-to on the outskirts of the main complex. It had been very relaxing to be far away from the main theatre of war.

17

After the short journey to the dockside he was shown aboard the *Khedive Ismail* and allocated to his quarters. After exchanging a few words with some naval bods, who were sharing the same cabin, he ventured out on deck to witness the sun already high in the clear blue sky. The faint breeze seemed to intensify the rising temperature, promising a hot and oppressive day ahead. It was Friday, 4th February 1944. Security was unusually vigilant, as thousands of troops and personnel gathered in groups near the quayside, awaiting their instructions as to which ship to board for the journey to Colombo. Around the assemblies of servicemen and women lay the usual array of kitbags and personal belongings. As the morning wore on, each group of passengers was delegated to one of the five ships in the port.

During the early morning Bill Howard, a Leading Signalman and two Ordinary Signalmen were dispatched from KR8's ocean escort ship HMS *Hawkins* to SS *Khedive Ismail*. They joined the troopship from the seaward side, transported on the cruiser's motor launch. They were required to receive naval signals and ensure efficient communication between the four Royal Navy escorts and the Commodore's ship throughout the voyage (naval procedures were substantially different, in concept, to the merchant service). Whilst Bill was checking over the signal system he saw the 301st Field Regiment being marched over to the *Khedive Ismail*, while infantry from the King's African Rifles joined other ships berthed along the busy quayside. They were apparently very apprehensive about joining the ship and a majority were housed below decks in the fo'c's'le and stern hold areas, normally used for cargo. A lot of them refused to go below and remained on the upper decks throughout the voyage. (Apparently, the evening before they had boarded the ship, some of the African troops had gone to the local cinema only to be confronted with some newsreel footage, showing ships being sunk in convoy.)

Lieutenant-Colonel J. A. Stevens, OBE, who commanded the 301st Regiment (formerly known as the 1st) explained, in a later report, that the regiment was formed at Larkhill, Kenya, in July 1942 and consisted initially of HQ and 57th Battery. In December of the same year it embarked for Madagascar, where 56th Battery, which had fought against the Vichy forces, came under command. Meanwhile the third battery (62nd) was being raised in Kenya.

The Regiment returned to Kenya in May 1943 for leave and training before setting off to form part of the 11th East African Divisional Artillery, which was being acclimatised in Ceylon for service in Burma. One of its last public engagements, before leaving Kenya, was a demonstration of firing a barrage and a series of concentrations over the heads of an advancing battalion of King's African Rifles at Naivasha. The askari did not put a foot (or a round) wrong and all were confident that they would not let down their infantry in battle.

The Regiment, close on a thousand strong, boarded HMT *Khedive Ismail* with the exception of the second-in-command and the battery subalterns, who boarded another ship in the same convoy.

Gloria West, who was one of the nine recruits from the Women's Territorial Service, remembered being issued with identification papers before boarding the ship. They each carried their own personal luggage whilst their heavy luggage had been transported from Nairobi on a separate train. They filed up the gangway with the nurses and the 301st Regiment, who were the last to board the ship. The troopship appeared to be full to capacity. (Although all the WTS members onboard were listed as an East African Unit, there were two recruits from the United Kingdom; Barbara Kentish and Florence Moojen.)

In addition to the *Khedive Ismail*, there were three other ships owned by the British India Steam Navigation Company: the *Ellenga*, *Ekma* and *Varsova* and a fifth which was owned by the Ellerman Lines and named *City of Paris*. All five similar ships were destined for the same convoy, a troop-carrying exercise coded KR8.

Buster's quarters were on the upper deck towards the after end of the main accommodation, on the port side. The cabin was reasonably sized and provided just enough space to billet eight Petty Officers, including himself. He was made very welcome and stowed the small amount of his belongings by the only remaining bunk. The alleyway was still thronging to the sound of latecomers trying to locate their appointed compartments prior to departure whilst the familiar smell of baking bread drifted around the ship, reminding everyone that it would soon be time for lunch.

In the meantime the women of the WTS were shown to their three small cabins which were shared equally, three to a room. Their bunk beds were tiered above one another and everyone excitedly compared each others quarters. Next door to Gloria's cabin was a naval officer, his wife and a baby boy. At lunchtime they were directed to the side dining room which had been allocated for the explicit use of the female passengers, with the exception of two tables which had been reserved for men.

Once the complement was concluded the gangway was lifted, and the ship manoeuvred into the bay of the scenic harbour where she anchored. After lunch, Buster spent some time settling into his cabin and getting to know some of the other occupants. That evening he lazed about on the promenade deck and joined in a convivial sing-song before retiring to his hot and humid quarters.

For the benefit of the officers and women, a talk on lifeboat procedures was carried out in the lounge, whereupon everybody present was issued with a lifebelt which they were instructed to take with them at all times. They were shown how to wear them and what to do in case they had to jump overboard. They were then taken onto the boat deck where, together with the Africans, they were allocated to a specific lifeboat should the need arise.

This crucial exercise was carried out daily, to familiarise everyone with the important drill and expedite its implementation should it be deemed necessary at any time during the voyage. However, it should also be pointed out that the lowering procedure took several minutes even when the ship was on an even keel. The passengers were not embarked until the lifeboat had been swung out and lowered to the boat deck level. Loading was never carried out during boat drill so, in a real emergency situation when time was of the essence, the confusion and panic usually resulted in a disorganised scramble to the wrong boat. Invariably, sinking ships never conformed to practice conditions and varied in angles of submergence. In any case, lifeboats were never lowered down to water-level whilst ships were at sea because of the weather conditions and probable risk of damage. Therefore, most of the ship's officers were not proficient with the whole procedure and if the responsible dutyman failed to arrive at his lifeboat station, due to injury, there was, more often than not, no suitable replacement to take over. Another important consideration was the possible malfunction of some of the davit equipment in an emergency. Although the captains ordered regular boat drills, both the officers and passengers never knowingly realised their importance, believing that the bizarre situation would never happen to them. Consequently, they often found the whole task a perfunctory chore, necessary only because they were ordered to do so.

High-water was just before three o'clock in the afternoon. The *Hawkins* moved slowly past them with a large contingent of her crew neatly lining the main deck. If their movements had been secret up to now, the musical talents of the old cruiser's band loudly announced the commencement of the impending voyage with one of the wartime favourites, 'Over There'. The cruiser negotiated the harbour entrance along with the corvette *Honesty* and the anti-submarine cutters *Sennen* and *Lulworth*, clearing the boom by 13.40 local time (3 hours ahead of GMT). The steamships *Khedive Ismail, Varsova*, the sisterships *Ekma* and *Ellenga* and lastly, the 10,902 ton

City of Paris followed the escort into the open sea. Once clear of the harbour the ships formed into their pre-determined positions with the two A/S ships screening ahead and 30 degrees to port and starboard of the leading columns. The third escort ship, HMS *Honesty*, covered the rear of the convoy. HMS *Hawkins* led the port column. A course of 149° was set, at a speed of 10 knots, but the speed was gradually worked up to 13 knots as each ship adjusted to her mandatory position.

The five transports were carrying just over six thousand Army troops and personnel (6,311 to be exact) along with personal kit and small arms (which were stored under lock and key in case of accidents). There were 19 officers from the 301st Field Regiment who were originally designated to the *Khedive Ismail,* but, due to the absence of suitable quarters, they were detached to a different ship before sailing.

The *Khedive Ismail* was carrying a complement of 1,511 people including 996 officers and men of the 301st Field Regiment, 271 Royal Navy personnel (including 19 Wrens), 178 Ship's crew, one matron with 53 nursing sisters and 9 members of the Women's Territorial Service. She also carried one war correspondent and a naval officer's wife and 5-month-old son. The Army contingent were being shipped eastwards to strengthen the 11th East African Division in readiness to support the Burma Campaign which had commenced earlier that year. The nursing sisters were required to staff the 150th General Hospital, serving the Army requirements as and when they would be needed. The Wrens were to be deployed for communication and administrative duties within the Royal Navy shore establishments in Ceylon, whilst the WTS were to be utilised assisting the hospital services. Most of the Royal Naval personnel were to attend HMS *Lanka* ready for drafting.

During the morning of the 6th the sea became quite choppy and the absence of a few of the more familiar faces showed that the journey was already claiming the first sufferers of sea-sickness.

It had been decided prior to departure, by Captain R. C. Whiteman, who was acting as commodore on board the *Khedive Ismail*, that the convoy would not plot a zig-zag course because this would imply an extra night at sea, partly because of the greater distance (the zig-zag would add many miles to the journey) and partly because the port of Colombo was closed throughout the night. The alternative strategy had been recommended by the captain of *Hawkins*, John William Josselyn. He had backed down, but had insisted that, should it at any time on the voyage become advisable, zig-zag numbers 12 and 38 were to be implemented.

The zig-zag strategy helped make a ship a more difficult target, even if spotted by a submarine. It was hoped that, should a U-boat begin an attack, the regular and unpredictable change of course would spoil the submarine's approach to its target. Once a submarine had submerged its effective speed and range of vision were greatly reduced, meaning that it usually only had one chance to make a successful kill. Even if a U-boat had spotted a ship it could easily lose it again because the periscope could never protrude far out of the water. At different stages of the War, alternative strategies were experimented with, such as convoys without zig-zag, or ships sailing without convoy. It was difficult in war conditions to tell which strategy best avoided the threat of submarine attack. However, towards the end of hostilities the Admiralty had circulated instructions recommending that all convoys were to zig-zag over 11 knots.

At 11.04, the speed of the convoy was reduced to 12½ knots to allow *Varsova* to regain station whereupon, less than two hours later, the convoy's course was altered to 81° and the speed was restored to 13 knots. The first day passed uneventfully.

On the morning of February 7th there was very little breeze, just a gentle swell that everyone was getting used to. Buster felt that he had once again regained his sea-legs even though he had not been exactly 'one hundred per cent' the day before and he was still hobbling along with a leg in plaster. As the sun rose above the eastern horizon the group of ships altered their course corrections in unison to 73°.

Mr K. C. Gandar-Dower, who was then a war correspondent and wanted to get some ideas for an article he was writing on the Regiment, offered a prize for the best letter written by an African. It produced some amusing results. One askari had the idea that the ship ran along rails hidden under the water; others were convinced that the *sindano* (the needle used for cholera inoculation) was the complete cure for sea-sickness. It so happened that the injections were conducted just about the time they had got their sea legs.

It was during this calm morning that Buster took the chance to look around this fine old ship, to learn a little about her design and history. He walked about her and noted that her forward third had two small hatches which, in more peaceful times, would have stored a reasonable amount of cargo. At this point in time, however, the upper, main and orlop decks from No. 1 hatch forward to the forecastle were being used to house some of the East African troops. The hatch covers were boarded but not battened down so as to enable the tarpaulin covers to be rolled back. The four wooden corner sections were then removed to assist ventilation to the decks below. The only access was through two watertight entrances on the port and starboard sides of the well-deck, whilst the lower decks were connected by twelve-foot-wide steel stairways. Straw palliasses were placed next to each other in regular lines of conformity, necessary to provide enough sleeping space for this large contingent of troops. The East African officers were supplied with steel bunks, which were bolted to the deck. It was not hard to imagine the stifling conditions that they had to endure during this voyage, at the height of summer. Added to the partial hatch openings (previously described) were a dozen portholes each side of the ship (on the main deck only) and several movable deck vents, with canvas extensions, which provided minimal air movement to the decks below. The intervening hatch spaces beneath were covered by manageable steel hatchbeams that facilitated the support and location of large wooden hatchboards. At the after end of No. 1 hatch, on the main deck, a sizable bolted bulkhead section had been removed to utilise the useful space that No. 2 hatch provided for more, similar, accommodation.

Directly in front of the forward mast was a sampson post which supported a small hydraulic crane; another crane was situated between the two entrances on the well-deck aft of No. 2 hatch. Two carley floats which were supported on steel angular structures were situated either side of the well deck (as were two more on the after deck). The main accommodation rose vertically, five decks, to an open bridge which was above another covered bridge which also incorporated the wireless and chartroom. This area also accommodated the deck and engineering officers, on the same level as the boat deck, where eight lifeboats were neatly stowed, four each side. Because the troopship was carrying approximately six times the complement she was designed for (originally she would have carried just under two hundred and fifty passengers, plus the ship's crew) an additional 36 rafts had been stowed, behind the after bulkhead of the officers' accommodation. Buster felt that the large funnel, which raked slightly aft in line with her two masts, gave her a pleasing profile. Two fidley spaces (air spaces covered with steel gratings) in front and behind the funnel, along with four very large vents, provided the intake of forced-air required to aspirate her oil-fired boilers. Behind these, and above a former gymnasium (now used for recreational purposes), four further vents and a skylight provided air to the engine room whilst several smaller intakes provided some movement of air through to the various cabin and hold spaces, unfortunately at the same temperature as its source.

The promenade deck was used for various utility purposes and included a main lounge, reading and recreation rooms and was complemented with a small shop. Below this were the two main accommodation areas; the bridge deck which, on this voyage, housed most of the senior officers, and the upper deck which berthed a number of the British Army, Naval and female personnel. This was the only deck with port-holes, but the two decks above did have large brass rectangular windows, which pivoted from two hinges at one end and were dogged with two brass, swivelling, screwed handles at the other. They opened inboard allowing some air movement, as and when required. From the forward upper deck to the main lounge, two decks above, a large double balustraded staircase ascended and converged to a wider central stairway. The stairwell was tastefully enriched with delicate inlays of marquetry set in the large wooden panels. Sizable mirrors helped to disclose the former grandeur of this once eminent liner. The staircase led passengers into a spacious lounge that still housed a semi-circular, and elevated, stage at one end. It was not difficult to imagine a resident band playing music to passengers in expensive evening wear; at this current time, however, it was being used for reading, letter writing, card and board games and the occasional concert: becoming one of the most eagerly sought areas of the ship in the daylight hours.

At the other end of the forward staircase, on the upper deck, was the dining-room which was entered through two French doors. No expense had been spared in the stateliness of this area either. It was not hard to visualise the peacetime captain sat at the head of the room, whilst the affluent passengers awaited the arrival of various exquisite dishes which they could select and cut using silver-plated cutlery; placed either side of bone-china crockery, richly embellished with fancy napkins and flower arrangements; the resident pianist entertaining the guests with soft music, whilst the waiters poured the wines chosen by each table. The adequate galley would have provided 'cordon bleu' menus of the highest standard, but now it only catered for the basic food requirements of a large number of troops in wartime. Another smaller dining room was situated on the starboard side just behind the former. Most of the occupants were sub-divided into groups of a half-dozen or so, and a pre-selected messman queued for their meals, collecting them in aluminium dixies, which slotted into a special circular holder. It was then shared out and eaten wherever they could find a suitable space. Most of the officers used the large saloon area, whilst all the women used the small dining room opposite the ship's galley. Most of the subordinates used the spaces in the hold or even ate out on deck. Viewing the ship from the exterior, the larger portholes gave the only clue as to the saloon's position.

Behind the main accommodation were two smaller holds, again housing more African troops in cramped conditions similar to those of the forward section of the ship. These were divided by a stouter mast and masthouse through which the occupants of the after hold spaces could gain access, by means of several water-tight entrances around its small rectangular structure. A high after-poop deck housed the one hundred and thirty members of the crew and, on either side of this accommodation were two more lifeboats. Directly below, on the main deck, the majority of the naval consignment were billeted; whilst a dozen or so port-holes provided some air movement and, more often than not, boasted a cleverly devised air-scoop made from either cardboard or a suitable piece of jointing material, creating a welcome draught should wind conditions be favourable. This deck was an open-plan affair with interspersed steel stanchions supporting the smaller accommodation above it. At the outset of the voyage, Bill Howard along with his two junior counterparts, all from HMS *Hawkins*, had been originally instructed to bed down in this same area. After brief explanations, concerning their need to maintain a twenty-four-hour watch for sending and receiving important naval signals, they were soon re-allocated to a small cabin on the port side of the main accommodation, adjoining three other similar sized cabins which housed most of the junior ranks of the Women's Royal Naval Service.

Her hull and superstructure was painted mid-grey, a standard wartime livery commonly used by the Admiralty for all cargo and troopships worked in eastern waters. For the main part she was rivetted together, with the occasional weld which was difficult to detect under the liberal coats of paint. The promenade and boat decks were embellished with teak planking which was laid in and separated by a thin sandwich of bitumen, to allow for both waterproofing and expansion and contraction from changes in temperature. These were hosed down early in the mornings, and periodically 'holy-stoned' (treated with a fine sand to scour the decks).

The *Khedive Ismail* was no different to any other standard troopship as regards armament and protection. She carried six 20mm oerlikon guns which were mounted in special pods on the forward upper deck, outer bridge and after boat deck. A 12-pounder was situated above the after crew accommodation whilst a 4-inch low-angle gun was similarly placed on the next deck down. A steel canopy was welded just above the bridge windows whilst some of the nugatory portholes and windows were plated, giving some protection from possible aerial attack.

In the early hours of Wednesday, 9th February, the three escorting ships departed, as planned, because they did not carry sufficient fuel for the whole journey. Replacements were already on their way from the east but, for the time being, the convoy relied solely for protection on the vigilance of the cruiser, HMS *Hawkins*, which had positioned herself centrally ahead of the convoy and was carrying out a broad zig-zag, whilst the troopships maintained a steady course (*Hawkins* had no ASDIC facilities). At 08.42 (convoy or local time) the Commodore made a signal to the convoy that loud receiver oscillations could be heard, from the south-east, on a wave-length of 600 metres. As the ships continued in a north-westerly direction the signal grew weaker. There was no further explanation or investigation into the matter.

As the last rays of the setting sun faded, the ships went into black-out to prevent their being spotted by the enemy. The phenomenon known as phosphorescence was observed by some of the passengers. (This is caused by swarms of minute protozoa which emit light, rather like glow worms or fireflies, illuminating the disturbed sea with myriads of tiny luminary flashes.) This natural wonder could be (and was on this journey) used to good advantage to keep convoy ships in station. A cleverly designed open-ended construction made from steel, and not unlike an old box kite to look at, except that there were large vented holes at the front and top, would be towed behind the leading ships. The resulting phosphorescent trail, left by its scooping and dumping action, was fairly easy to follow and, with practice, enabled the following ships to keep in line and at a reasonable distance. In the case of convoy KR8, the foremost ships also signalled a single recognition letter to the ships astern of them. Messages were sent by the use of a long torch with a blue lamp; a button on the opposite end enabled the duty signalman to send his Morse Coded sign, on the hour, every hour. Use of radio was kept to a minimum because of the possibility that messages could be intercepted by the enemy. (Aldis lamps were not used at night for obvious reasons.)

The following day, *Hawkins* contacted *Khedive Ismail* and a brief conference between the two captains concerning the application of zig-zag manoeuvres was, once again, deferred without an agreed change of plan. During mid-morning, *Khedive Ismail* slowed astern of the convoy under a flurry of thick black smoke, a dead give-away to any enemy submarines, surface ships or aircraft close to the area. The situation was soon rectified when a stand-by boiler fan was put on-line and the appropriate adjustments made. Within an hour she had resumed her station and the convoy speed was resumed at 13 knots.

Friday, 11th February passed peacefully, except that convoy KR8 crossed the equator at 21.00. At about the same time, some of the passengers and crew witnessed a spectacular display of lightning and could hear the distant rumble of thunder as the convoy skirted the vicinity of a tropical storm, southwards of their position. The dark clouds and setting sun created a dramatic backdrop as several independent waterspouts gyrated large vortices of sea-water upwards, until their eventual connection with clouds almost vertically above them. Course changes were introduced to avoid the storm, but the sea became somewhat rougher and the wind grew much stronger and cooler.

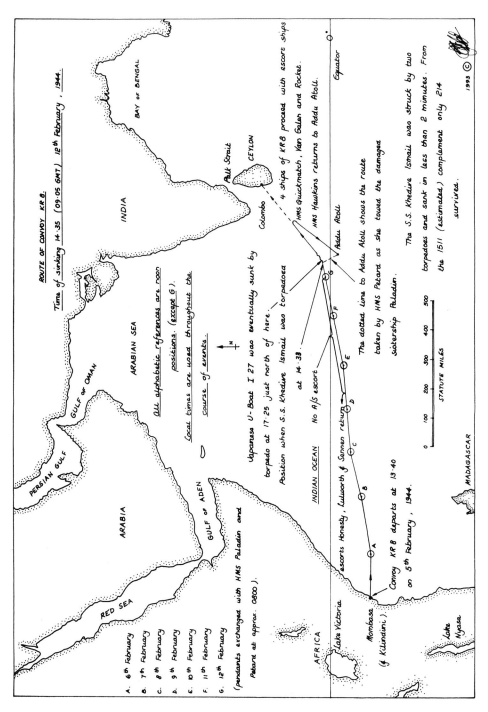

ROUTE OF CONVOY KR 8.

Time of sinking 14·35 (09·05 GMT) 12th February, 1944.

All alphabetic references are noon positions. (except G).

Local times are used throughout the course of events.

Japanese U-Boat I 27 was eventually sunk by torpedo at 17·25 just north of here.

Position when S.S. Khedive Ismail was torpedoed at 14·33.

INDIAN OCEAN   No A/s escort

4 ships of KR8 proceed with escort ships
HMS Quickmatch, Van Galen and Racket.
HMS Hawkins returns to Addu Atoll.

Addu Atoll

The dotted line to Addu Atoll shows the route taken by HMS Petard as she towed the damaged sistership Paladin.

The S.S. Khedive Ismail was struck by two torpedoes and sank in less than 2 minutes. From the 1511 (estimated) complement only 214 survived.

escorts Honesty, Lulworth & Sennen return

Convoy KR 8 departs at 13·40 on 5th February, 1944.

A. 6th February
B. 7th February
C. 8th February
D. 9th February
E. 10th February
F. 11th February
G. 12th February

(pendants exchanged with HMS Paladin and Petard at approx. 0800).

BAY OF BENGAL

INDIA

Palk Strait

Colombo   CEYLON

ARABIAN SEA

GULF OF OMAN

PERSIAN GULF

ARABIA

GULF OF ADEN

RED SEA

AFRICA

Lake Victoria
Mombasa
(& Kilundini).

Lake Nyasa

MADAGASCAR

STATUTE MILES
0   100   200   300   400   500

Equator

1993 ©

12. Route of convoy KR8.

III

THE SINKING OF SS *KHEDIVE ISMAIL*

As dawn broke on Saturday morning, 12th February 1944, it revealed a clear blue sky, a calm sea and the customary hot sun. Lookouts soon observed a ship far on the south-eastern horizon and by 08.04 (local time) they had exchanged pendants with HMS *Petard* and, six minutes later, with HMS *Paladin.* This lifted the morale of many passengers who felt the added reassurance of their protection. (The two P class destroyers should have been accompanied by HMS *Penn* but she had developed defects and was unable to proceed from Colombo, rendering her unoperational for this particular convoy.) The *Paladin* took station 30° on the port bow of the convoy with *Petard* similarly positioned on the starboard side. Both of the destroyers immediately adopted a broad zig-zag ahead of the three leading ships using their ASDIC sets to search the sea ahead.

The ships in the convoy were now positioned three cables apart both ahead and abeam (1,800 feet, about one-third of a mile). They were in three columns, with *Hawkins* in front of the port column, *Khedive Ismail* leading the centre and the 4,701-ton *Varsova* (Captain John Walton Knight) leading the starboard column. Behind these, in similar order, were (port to starboard) *City of Paris* (Captain Herbert Percival), *Ekma* (5,108 tons, Vice Commodore, Captain Denis Gun-Cuninghame) and, finally, *Ellenga* (5,196 tons, Captain Robert Brodie Clark).

* * *

As the morning wore on Buster hobbled up the stairway, still in his plaster cast, and went aft of the boat deck. From this vantage point he watched the other ships following in neat formation. The *Paladin* and *Petard* were approximately two miles ahead slowly zig-zagging, ever probing for the enemy. The sea surface was milky-smooth with sporadic capfuls of wind disturbing and rippling the surface. The convoy was now about sixty miles south-west of the One and Half Degree Channel, the widest passage through the southern Maldive Island group between Hadhdhunmathee Atoll and the more southerly North Huvadhoo Atoll.

29

13. The 9,800 ton cruiser HMS *Hawkins* in 1942 (she was built in 1917).

14. The SS *City of Paris*, built in 1922 for Ellerman's Indian and South African services (she originally had accommodation for 250 passengers).

15. An aerial view of SS *City of Paris* passing the coastline of Cape Town.

16. SS *Ellenga* (seen here in British India Line's colours).

17. SS *Ekma*, sister ship to the SS *Ellenga.*

18. The troopship SS *Varsova.*

19. The *Khedive Ismail* photographed before the outbreak of war.

* * *

Buster looked at his watch and realised it was time for lunch. After he had finished his meal he decided to retire to his berth for an afternoon siesta, a decision that the other members of his cabin had almost duplicated in unison. From just forward of them and two levels above, on the promenade deck, the soft musical sounds of a concert, which was being held in the main lounge, broke the accustomed and reassuring noises of a ship at sea; whilst revictualled occupants pattered down the port alleyway to relax in the confines of their quarters. Others read books or wrote letters home, whilst a few leant on handrails or sat down on the open decks, whiling away the time with idle chat. The signallers amused themselves by reading the messages being passed from ship to ship by lamp.

The concert party had been well publicised and attracted an audience of white NCOs from the Army, Navy and female complement and had been organised by Captain Peter Croyden. It was being conducted by anyone who was talented enough to perform, both male and female. The time was after 14.00 and, judging from the rapturous applause, the concert was well attended. On the after deck a game of Tombola (Bingo) had begun, also attracting a number of people.

* * *

Signalman Bill Howard had finished his watch duties at 14.00 and made his way back to his cabin when, on arriving outside in the alleyway, he came upon a group of Wrens who were sharing several open tins of fruit they had presumably purchased from the small shop. They offered him some of the contents which he graciously declined as he squeezed past to enter his berth. As he took off his coat he could hear someone's suggestion to go up onto the boat deck to relax and sunbathe. The proposal was unanimously approved with the exception of one, who quietly explained that she wanted to retire to her cabin for a lie down, as she had previously had a restless night.

* * *

In the meantime, Buster had drifted into a deep sleep on top of the mess table, assisted by the slow motion of the ship. Below the two open port-holes of the cabin, the familiar sound of the sea could be faintly heard fizzing past the ship's hull, as if annoyed by its bulk pushing it aside into a frothing, diminishing wake. The slightest breeze irregularly ruffled the aftermost curtains which sometimes whisped, fleetingly, across one of the brows of the perspiring occupants, offering a brief reprieve from the humid, airless conditions of the austere accommodation. Deep in the bowels of the unseen engine room, the reassuring whine of the steam turbines was faintly discernible, confirming that all was well. The serenity from within the berth was slightly disturbed by the gentle creaking of the wooden decor in the casual swell.

* * *

At 14.33 (09.03 GMT), the peace was shattered by a deep explosion in the centre of the ship. The *Khedive Ismail* shook to the impact and immediately started to list to starboard; seconds later another, more violent, explosion erupted deep in the heart of the grand old liner. She had received two torpedo hits in the engine and boiler rooms respectively and continued to heel rapidly to starboard. The situation was extremely serious.

* * *

Buster and Petty Officer Turner (there were two POs by the name of Turner onboard – one did not survive. See Appendices) made for the two open portholes; by now the ship was on her beam ends, deepening by the stern and starting to break in half with both the bows and the stern slowly lifting out of the water independently. After quickly wriggling through the small open porthole, Buster hobbled (one leg still in plaster) down the stricken ship's side, negotiated the rolling chock and, seeing a young woman hovering at the edge of the black barnacled hull, he and the other petty officer hooked their arms under hers and plunged headlong into the

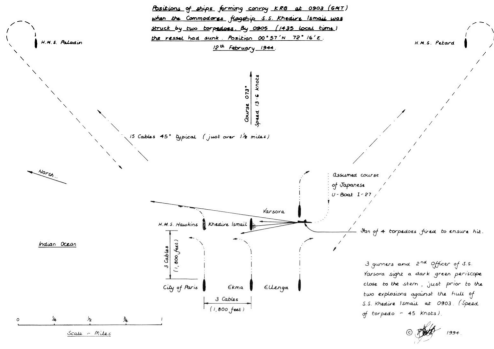

Positions of ships forming convoy KR8 at 0903 (GMT) when the Commodores flagship S.S. Khedive Ismail was struck by two torpedoes. By 0905 (1435 local time) the vessel had sunk. Position 00°57'N 72°16'E.
12th February. 1944.

H.M.S. Paladin

H.M.S. Petard

Course 073°
Speed 13·6 Knots

15 Cables 45° typical (just over 1½ miles)

North

Assumed course of Japanese U-Boat I-27

Varsova

Fan of 4 torpedoes fired to ensure hit.

Indian Ocean

H.M.S. Hawkins Khedive Ismail

3 Cables (1,800 feet)

City of Paris   Ekma   Ellenga

3 Cables (1,800 feet)

3 gunners and 2nd Officer of S.S. Varsova sight a dark green periscope close to the stern, just prior to the two explosions against the hull of S.S. Khedive Ismail at 0903. (Speed of torpedo - 45 Knots).

© 1994.

0   ¼   ½   ¾   1
Scale - Miles

20. Positions of all ships in convoy KR8 at the time of the torpedo attack.
21. Sketch of the first torpedo hit on the *Khedive Ismail* with *City of Paris* and *Ekma* in the background.

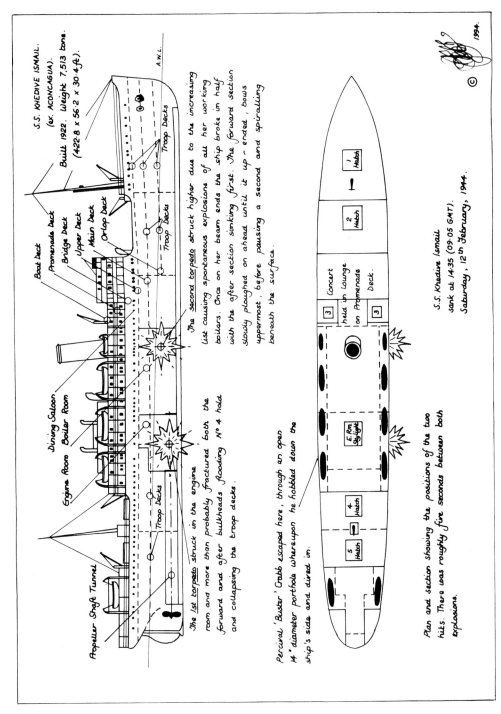

22. Plan and side elevation of the troopship *Khedive Ismail* showing the positions of impact of both torpedoes.

23. Photograph of an oil painting by Bristolian artist Robert Blackwell depicting the *Khedive Ismail* being struck by the second torpedo. She had already started to list to starboard after the first incursion some seconds earlier.

turbulent sea. The ship continued moving forward and, in the corner of his eye, he remembered seeing the port propeller still rotating. When he surfaced, the ship had already disappeared, leaving a few scattered survivors, lifeboats, rafts and wreckage. Above, where the ship had once been, hung a large yellow, sulphurous, cloud which drifted slowly in the almost cloudless, blue sky. The surface of the sea was frothing and erupting as flotsam, fuel oil and air broke away from the mortally damaged troopship making its 12,000-feet descent to the bottom.

* * *

By now, he had swum to a green smoke canister and, hanging onto this, took stock of the situation. There were several survivors either swimming or hanging on to whatever floated. In a very short space of time the *Ekma* passed by, quite close to the submerged quarry and survivors, both black and white: some dead, some alive and some shouting for help. As the troopship glided past, some of the crew members threw lifebuoys over the side to assist those fortunate enough to survive the rapid submergence. But they did not stop.

It was obvious, with a submarine still in the vicinity, that all the other troopships and their 4,500 remaining passengers should get as far away from the scene as quickly and safely as possible. As the convoy dispersed, the vulnerable survivors were left to their own devices and those still swimming sought the refuge of anything that floated. Buster and Bill Howard were, independently, certain that the submarine passed under them as there was quite a turbulence of water with an apparent wake behind it. Some 200 yards away from them were two lifeboats from the ship, one was upright with little freeboard whilst the other was upside down; several survivors swam towards them.

Hawkins sailed away with the troopships, and *Petard* and *Paladin* moved in to deal with the submarine.

* * *

Just prior to the fatal incident three gunlayers belonging to the Maritime Royal Artillery – Cliff Horrell, Ted Barber and Bill Jackson – standing on the stern gun platform on *Varsova*, and their 2nd Officer – Stephen Dexter, who had been alerted by the starboard bridge-wing lookout – had seen the submarine's dark green periscope protruding some three feet above the surface. When first sighted it was about 50 feet from under her stern, on the starboard edge of the wake and travelling at about 4 knots in a direction Green 135° to Red 45°, towards the *Khedive Ismail*. In fact, it was so close that the gunners could not depress their gun far enough to open fire. The submarine fired four torpedoes at a range of approximately 600 yards which, at 45 knots, would have taken barely 25 seconds to reach their target.

* * *

Cliff Horrell remembers that the first torpedo struck in line with her third and fourth lifeboats, deep in the heart of the engine room. It was followed, seconds later, by the second torpedo which struck directly below her funnel causing a catastrophic chain-reaction as the working boilers detonated instantaneously and with an intensity that could only spell disaster.

* * *

A soldier, who was washing up on the top of No. 4 hold on board the afflicted ship, saw the hatch covers blown upwards and the ladder collapse, whilst the troop decks and stairways below them suffered a similar fate, compounding the inevitable high loss of life. The final, colossal, explosion literally blew the bottom out of the vessel and the upward eruption of flying metal not only holed the boat deck, but destroyed the main stairway and collapsed some of the forward troop decks, trapping a great number of personnel on the upper deck and hold spaces below them. As the ship turned onto her beam ends, she began to sink by the stern and break in half. The sea poured into the broken sections of the ship, forced in by her own momentum, finding its way into the open hatches, portholes, fidley gratings and skylights, accelerating her rapid submergence. Those watching or participating in the concert had little chance of survival, but two who did survive said that the music had attracted an audience of over three hundred people. As soon as the second torpedo tore into the boiler room the furniture, including a grand piano, slid down the angled deck, accelerating and pinning many occupants against the starboard bulkhead. On the whole there were too many passengers, there were too few escape routes (as the windows only opened from the sides with some probably dogged down and, unlike a porthole, hardly provided any extra escape routes) and the ship sank too quickly for them to have any hope of escape.

* * *

Despite these adverse odds, one survivor, Bill Howard (a leading signalman on loan from HMS *Hawkins*) came out of his cabin and turned left (inboard) towards the main alleyway. He had barely made two steps towards the already obscured interior when his foot failed to touch the envisaged deck, which must have been destroyed only seconds before. In almost total darkness he quickly reversed his direction and headed outboard, along the only other escape route available to him. Through the acrid and choking smoke he could barely define the familiar shape of an open porthole. As soon as he reached it he was confronted by a dazed Wren who appeared,

24. Leading Signalman Bill Howard, RN,
who was on loan from HMS *Hawkins*.

25. Leading Wren Mrs Norah Munro,
RN, whom Bill Howard saved.

quite suddenly, through a canvas curtain next to the aperture. Bill quickly told her to hold onto him whilst he wriggled through the brass opening. By now the ship was on her beam ends with Bill outside the porthole and pulling the Wren behind him, but her semi-inflated life-jacket made it difficult to squeeze her through; instinctively, he refused to release her grip and they both started to descend beneath the ocean with the ship. Their death was as certain as anything could be in such chaos, but fate intervened. The air pressure in the ship was building up and a sudden eruption of air pushed her through the porthole and most of the way to the surface. They found themselves alongside an upturned lifeboat. Unfortunately a surface-bound piece of wood struck her on the head causing a very large contusion. Her name was Mrs Norah Munro and her subsequent refusal to be parted from his company only manifested her full appreciation of his selfless bravery.

* * *

Petty Officer Walker's story, although the numbers quoted are inaccurate, appeared in the *Melbourne Herald* in the 1960s. He had served in the Royal Navy for 25 years before joining the the Royal Australian Navy as a Chief Petty Officer gunnery instructor in 1953. The paper recorded his experience on that fateful day:

> ... Our first stop was Southampton, and we sailed in the *Orbita*. As each day at sea went by we hoped the veil of secrecy would be lifted. But no, even to this day I had no idea where we were really going. When we entered the Mediterranean our imaginations ran riot, but we steamed steadily on, through the Suez Canal, into the Red Sea and down the East African coast to Mombasa. There we disembarked. Members of all the other units onboard went to their respective barracks. But the naval contingent went under canvas. Three weeks later we went aboard the *Khedive Ismail*. Little did the cheery company of officers, men, women and children aboard realise what lay in store. The *Khedive Ismail* and four other troopships sailed with an escort of four, including the cruiser *Hawkins*. When duties were assigned to the troops I was made WRNS instructor and it was due to this job that I survived.
>
> February 12th dawned beautiful and sunny, the sea was calm, and until that day, no ships had been sunk in our area, so all was well. During the morning I drilled the Wrens, and when I dismissed them, 21-year-old Leading Wren Pamela Wylie, of London, asked if I would lend her the book on field training. I told her I would bring it to her at 2.30 pm.
>
> That afternoon 400 of the ship's passengers crowded into the main lounge on the promenade deck for a concert; others were at Tombola in the after deck and some were in their cabins. On the naval mess deck, at the stern, sailors were having a siesta. A few passengers were up on the upper deck. At 2.30 pm I left our mess deck to deliver the book to Pamela Wylie. As I passed through reading rooms, I saw people playing cards, reading or writing letters which were destined never to be posted. The promenade deck was deserted when I arrived at the petty officer's alloted space, but sounds of hilarity and gaiety came from the main lounge where the concert was in full swing.
>
> Pamela Wylie came on deck and walked towards me. The time was 2.32 pm. Our hour had come, but there was no warning of immediate danger. A minute later a terrific explosion shattered the ship's stern. More explosions followed in quick succession. Laughter and peace had gone. In its stead came shouting, the smashing of glass, the scream of escaping steam, the cries of injured. For the *Khedive Ismail* had been the target for Japanese torpedoes. The submarine commander who had trained his sights on our ship had done his job only too well. The ship was finished. Her

bows came out of the water as the stern dipped and keeled her over to starboard. There was no time for boat drill, at which we had become experts. There was barely time for anything.

I pushed Leading Wren Wylie up the steeply sloping deck, lifted her over the rail and scrambled over beside her. We both slid into the water as the *Khedive Ismail* took her final plunge. I was dragged under three times, struggling and fighting each time to get to the surface. The third time I nearly gave in. The sea boiled so viciously that I had no idea whether I was struggling towards the surface or trying to go down. When I finally broke clear the troopship had gone. So had Pamela Wylie. The terrific strain and suction had been too much for her. The time from the blast of the first torpedo to the plunge of the *Khedive Ismail* was 1 minute and 40 seconds, but I felt to have been in the water for hours.

As the sea calmed again I took stock. All that remained of the ship were two lifeboats upside down, two rafts and 23 people – 17 men and 6 women – were the only survivors. They included a naval officer, four nursing sisters, two WRNS, three petty officers, two army sergeants, two East African soldiers and nine AB's and signalmen. 1,240 had died. Of the four Petty Officers who had left Plymouth, the eldest, PO Alf Turner, had been killed. I had last seen him playing cards when I passed through the reading room. All 23 survivors got to the rafts and boats and the injured and the women were helped on to them. The rest stayed in the water and held onto the sides. One of the injured Wrens was an Australian girl with the surname Chessell. She had been hit by the mast of the *Khedive Ismail* as it sank. All the survivors accounted for, the thought uppermost in our minds was, what next? The convoy had altered course and steamed off at high speed. Nothing was in sight. Below us the submarine lurked. Would the captain surface and take us prisoners, or what?

* * *

Lieutenant-Colonel J. Stevens also survived:

... I was asleep in my cabin on the bridge deck when an explosion threw me out of my bed, breaking a rib in the process. I had just picked myself up when we were hit again. The sunlight was cut off by the volume of water which came down on us (I was told later that the funnel which was the wall of my bathroom had also caved in). I picked up my life-jacket and threw it around my neck – no time to put my arms through the slings or tie them. I went out on deck and saw an officer diving overboard; no one else was about. I wondered what I should do and then saw the ship had heeled over so far that the promenade deck, above me, was very nearly down to the water-line. I flopped over the rails into the water, which was then level with the deck, and swam.

When I looked round, the last few feet of the bows were disappearing. There had been no time to lower boats or throw off rafts, but one boat had launched itself the right way up and there was another upside down. I gained the former along with a naval rating, and we were soon joined by a naval officer and our regimental MO and others. We got hold of some oars and started to pull towards other survivors, picking up what we could in the way of water bottles and stores, a medical hamper, a sail and some spare oars. We soon had quite a number of survivors on board and could see others riding on an upturned boat and clinging to wreckage. Everyone behaved extremely well.

Those who did not get away (about 85%) must have had a very swift and merciful death, for of the thousand or so who lost their lives we found only two bodies. The naval officer and I dived in and brought these onboard where we tried ineffectually to bring them round with the MO's help and guidance. We understood that the ship disappeared completely in under two minutes. Those on the ship behind (the *Ekma*) later said there was nothing to see by the time they got on deck. Survival or not seemed to depend on the luck of the draw. There were escapes from all parts of the ship. The proportion of casualties was about even between the crew, the naval draft, the Regiment and the ladies. Two friends might be together until the last minute and one survive, the other not. The REME officer, Lieutenant Alexander Dunwoody, who was lost, went over with the Signal Officer, who survived. The Adjutant and clerk were shot out of the office, but the orderly was not. My African servant was not seen again, though he jumped with a friend who told the tale. Our QM, Owen, got caught up in the rigging and went down; but remembered his pension in time, and came up again. Two of the battery commanders, Roger Sharpley and Henry Head, were lost.

* * *

Phyllis Hutchinson, a nursing sister, relates her story:

... I was standing on the boat deck amidships, on the port side of the late ship *Khedive Ismail*, about to go down below to do some ironing on the afternoon of Saturday, February 12th 1944, when the first Japanese torpedo struck the vessel on the starboard side. The impact flung me forward on to the deck. There was a huge hole in the ship and I saw two of my friends disappear. The mast and the superstructure crashed, the ship rapidly developed a heavy list to starboard, thick smoke and debris obscured my view. I scrambled to my feet, grabbed a lifebelt slipping past me on the sloping deck and hastily donned it, hadn't time to fasten it properly when the second torpedo tore into the bows of the ship. Nobody near me to advise or help, a matter of seconds for the brain to realise that disaster had struck, instinctively I acted, jumping as far away from the ship

43

as possible, remembering to hold the front of my lifejacket to prevent it jerking my neck.

Flying debris must have struck the back of my head (as evidenced by a large egg-shaped swelling later). I was unaware of it and have no recollection of entering the sea. Later I came to and found myself deep in the ocean, being dragged down by a terrific suction, rather like being in the grip of a giant octopus, I did not feel anything and was blissfully ignorant of the fact that I was drowning peacefully.

The dead body of a girl shooting past me partially restored my numbed senses, I was instantly aware of my danger, aware of the dark green gloom, the uncanny silence and the noiseless destruction of the great ship disintegrating in the water. My spirit rebelled against the whole ghastly affair, strangely enough I never thought of death although I was perilously near to it. I kicked out frantically and endeavoured to swim upwards. I was soon conscious of a strange suffocating feeling in my chest; most uncomfortable.

I suppose I must have been on the edge of a vacuum because suddenly the suction ceased and I shot upwards. A pale greenish-white patch above my head grew rapidly larger and then came the wonderful moment when my head rose above it and I saw the sun high up in the sky. I dazedly thought how odd it was that I had not associated the patch of light with the reflection of the sun on the water.

I floated for a short time, endeavouring to get a little air into my overtaxed lungs and to regain some strength, as I was very exhausted. Queer rumbling underwater explosions disturbed me and had a weird effect on my body, a kind of vibrant shakiness and a sickening feeling of insecurity. Again the instinct for self-preservation came to my rescue, objects came into focus again, an overturned boat about twenty yards away was the nearest solid thing. With a great effort I managed to swim to it and I shall for ever remember the wonderful thrill of touching something solid and substantial again, as I grasped the hard wood of the boat and my cheek rested against it. There were nine Africans and another member of the Royal Artillery on top of the keel, two of the Africans leaned over, placed their hands under my armpits and heaved me up. I collapsed across the keel, water cascading out of my nose and mouth, I idly thought how disgusting such a performance was in front of the Askari. Then I entered a peculiar state, time, past, present and future merged, I knew everything and I knew nothing, was unaware of physical pain or anything going on around me. As from a great distance I became conscious of the other sister calling my name, I was drowsy and didn't wish to be disturbed; the voice became clearer and I was aware of anxiety in the tone of it. I realised there were other human beings alive and to be considered, with a great effort of will I managed to reply that I was alright and so came back to life again.

Presently I pulled myself up into a sitting position and took stock of my surroundings, no trace of the *Khedive Ismail* except for a few bits of wreckage strewn over the sea, the cruiser and other merchant ships speeding away to the horizon. I looked at my watch – a Grana, shock-proof and water-proof – it had lived up to its reputation and was still going; five minutes had elapsed since the previous time I had looked at it on the boat deck and warned my friend it was time for us to go below to use the iron, it seemed quite unbelievable.

The Africans were calm and stoical, bewildered ebony figures. I assured them we should soon be picked up, badly needing reassurance on that point myself. One wisely asked how long it would take us to reach land!

We were picked up after a few hours and taken aboard a destroyer where we received the utmost kindness and attention, no tribute can be too great for the Royal Navy; it is magnificent.

* * *

Tom Fox, whom the present writer met fifty years and one day after the tragic incident, at the Wrens' Memorial Service in London, recorded his experience in a personal letter sent to me before we actually met. The relevant section read as follows:

> ... I arrived in Mombasa in late December 1943 and worked in the signal/wireless station as a coder until I was drafted aboard the *Khedive Ismail* for transfer to the wireless station in Colombo, Ceylon. Mombasa was, in those days, a beautiful unspoilt East African town with magnificent silver sandy beaches and the locals were a very jolly and friendly people. Although all of us there in the forces were very much aware of it being wartime, I am sure that most of us thoroughly enjoyed our stay in Mombasa. I can personally remember it being a very happy time and enjoying the super swimming parties on the beaches – but then who wouldn't have enjoyed such pleasurable times at 18 years of age? Needless to say it was with some disappointment when the draft orders were issued for us to leave Mombasa and move to Colombo where we would be assembled for Mountbatten's combined forces operation to retake Burma and other Japanese occupied territories.

> My recollection of the *Khedive Ismail* is that she was an old Egyptian liner and seemed to be a bit 'match woody' in its general construction. It had of course been converted into a troopship and on this particular trip was in fact the commodore of the convoy. I understand she was carrying approximately 2,200 personnel who were serving in the Navy, Wrens, Army

26. Ordinary Coder Tom Fox, RN, who was blown off the troopship by the second explosion.

and units of the Army nursing sisters. The ship appeared to be full and somewhat congested below decks - it was a pleasure to spend as much time on the upper decks as the weather conditions were excellent except for Friday the 11th February when we ran very close to a tropical storm – the lightning and sea turbulence on the horizon were truly spectacular – these stormy conditions appeared to remain with us for most of Friday night but from daybreak on the Saturday morning we had returned to clear skies and calm seas and the usual very hot sun.

The Saturday morning passed in the usual way on board a trooper and after the midday meal a very good friend (Geoff Binns who I had been with since joining the Royal Navy) and I sat out in the open on one of the upper decks – I can still see this very clearly in my memory as if it was today – two 18 year olds laughing and joking and thinking what a great life it was in the Navy and seeing the world!

Our world was shattered by a huge explosion and complete turmoil – I had no idea what had happened and I can only remember being hurled across the deck which had suddenly lurched from side to side at very steep angles – I was thrown about the deck and at one time I was pinned between some deck lockers unable to move for what seemed an eternity. The next thing I can remember was being violently thrown into the sea by what must have been a further explosion and floating around with an incredible amount of debris. I can recall that there were four or five of us in close proximity but can only assume that we must all have been semi-dazed from the explosions and the sinking. Nevertheless after what would have been a relatively short time, say ten minutes or so, we found some debris which we formed into a type of float and we managed to hold on and take stock of the position. I remember collecting some food tins that were breaking the surface and the sudden surge of adrenalin when a pole, which may have been a broom stick, shot out of the water a few feet away from me. For the briefest moment, I thought it was a periscope! As the *Khedive Ismail* was no longer to be seen we could only conclude that it had gone down as a result of a torpedo attack. I was later to learn that my good friend, Geoff, had not survived.

* * *

Seventeen-year-old Eddie Turner, who was an Ordinary Signalman, was also on the after deck, immediately behind the main accommodation, playing Tombola. He had previously noticed a young woman, who was sitting down talking to another female passenger. Beside them, in the shade, lay a small baby. After several games, Eddie had a winning card which was duly checked by an army corporal. His win of forty-seven shillings had barely been placed in his hand when the ship recoiled to the two explosions, the force of which blew him across to the port side of the troopship. He tried to grab the handrail but the deck was lifting and tilting so rapidly, upwards and to the starboard side, that he literally slid down to the after corner of the deck into the swirling water. At the same instant he could hear frantic screams which were abruptly quelled just before he entered the sea. His arm and neck were trapped between some wooden crates but 'lady luck' was still with him, because their buoyancy began to lift him towards the surface. Still underwater, and with his eyes wide-open, he saw a carley float making a faster ascent; he grabbed hold of a side rope and eventually broke the surface; he had been under water for approximately one minute. As he looked around he saw the bows of the *Khedive Ismail*, poised vertically, before they disappeared beneath the surging sea. It was about one hundred yards from where he had emerged.

As he savoured his remarkable escape, and sucked in lungfuls of sweet, fresh air, he noticed one of the screening destroyers steaming towards him and the other survivors in the water.

47

27. Ordinary Signalman Eddie Turner, RN, who grabbed the ropes of a carley float whilst underwater.

Although it is true to say that the rapid sinking of the ship accounted for the great loss of life, in a bizarre way it had the opposite effect on 22-year-old Dan Docwra. This was how he described his experience to the author in a letter sent in April 1994. (Sadly he died on December 13th 1994 but not before I met him personally in August of that year.)

... The day we were sunk everyone was looking forward to the concert that was to take place in the afternoon. I did not go, instead I got my head down on the mess deck stool. My mess was the furthest aft on the deck just above the waterline. All of a sudden the *Khedive Ismail* was torpedoed (this was all too familiar an experience for Dan, for he had been sunk on the ammunition supply boat *Navasha* in 1940 and again on the Dido class cruiser *Hermione* in the middle of June 1942). She must have heeled over to the starboard side because the first thing I knew was all the screaming and shouting and everything that was loose such as plates, cups, tins, knives, forks and anything not screwed down sliding over to the starboard side. This all seemed to be happening in minutes, which I found out later was

28. Marine Dan Docwra who was well and truly stuck in a porthole.

seconds. I clung onto the mess deck table which was screwed to the deck and bulkhead and the last porthole aft was just above my head. I reached up and managed to get my head and shoulders through. This was on the port side which was now well out of the water, as she was laying at a ninety degree list. I was stuck and could not get my hips out of the porthole. I was well and truly jammed, half in half out. She started to go down fast then and the force of the water slapped me against the ship's side. This bit is my own opinion: I think that the force of the after end going down trapped the air in the stern and popped me out like a cork out of a bottle. I left the skin from my hips in the porthole! I was a long way down by then and the wreckage from the ship was passing me in the water. I did not know if I was still going down or not, but was very thankful when I broke the surface. I was quite close to an upturned lifeboat that had most of its bottom blown out and must have been blown off the ship by the explosion (the buoyancy tanks had presumably remained intact, because it had stabilised at a reasonable level and was fairly high out of the water). I was the first one to climb onboard and then I pulled half-a-dozen others up, including one of the Wrens and a South African nurse. Then a young white soldier, who had broken his leg, was screaming out about a couple of hundred yards away, all by himself. I could not leave him, and so swam out to him, but was scared he would make a grab for me. So I told him to grab my foot and towed him back to the upturned lifeboat, but I could not get back onboard myself because it was nearly tipping over with people trying to get out of the water.

* * *

The 2nd radio officer, William Thomson, was on watch in the wireless room. He felt the ship shiver as she was struck by the first torpedo. The air was filled with flying glass and debris, causing people on the boat deck to seek whatever shelter they could. Within a few seconds of the first shock, the second explosion caused the ship to list alarmingly to starboard, at an angle of about 45 degrees. Realising that no purpose could be served by remaining, he clung to the door frame and heaved himself over the threshold and made his way to the boat deck. Gingerly clambering over a pell-mell of twisted steel plates, he was suddenly engulfed by the sea as the ship slid beneath the surface.

He was not a competent swimmer and he felt that his chances of survival were very slim, especially without a life-jacket. Nevertheless, he kicked and struggled frantically through the wreckage until he could just see the green, shimmering surface. He reached his goal and gulped in a lungful of air before being drawn down a second time. His second ordeal dragged him even deeper, causing him to swallow several mouthfuls of sea water but, though nearing exhaustion, he managed to make the surface. Before long he was able to clamber aboard a small raft and observe the awful scene. Near his one-man raft were a number of lifeboats and a fair amount of wreckage, all pretty well on the water line with other unfortunates, like himself, clinging to them. Dotted here and there, within 200 yards, were other little islands of survivors. By then, there was no sign of the troopship and the other ships of the convoy had scattered and were almost five miles away when he scanned the horizon for them.

* * *

Having reached the relative safety of a boat or a float, the enormity of the event began to take hold of the thoughts of the few survivors. So many people, well over a thousand, had been cruelly taken, and in such a short time. It seemed unreal, like a dream, not least because of the tranquillity and calm around them. Everyone left in the water experienced a sense of desolation and a natural sense of vulnerability which would stay with them for some time to come.

From the onlookers on both the *Varsova*, which was only about 100 yards ahead of station and 3 cables (600 yards) abeam, the ship sank in 45 seconds. It has been difficult to specify the exact time that the ship took to sink as the reports do vary, but the longest reported time is no more than one minute, forty seconds (the time taken from the first explosion to the disappearance of the ship).

Although the periscope was reportedly observed by the Officer-of-the-Watch, Lieutenant Robert de Pass of *Petard*, it was too late; at that same moment the first torpedo exploded against the liner's pregnable hull. Immediately alarm bells rang, combined with the whooping sound of *Paladin*'s siren (six short blasts), every member of the well-trained ships' crews ran to their action stations and damage control positions as both ships sliced through the water with increasing speed and list, anxiously retracing their former position where the *Khedive Ismail* was leading the centre column. Straining eyes probed the sea ahead as the breeches of the 4-inch guns slammed shut in preparation for any imminent action. Below, in the ASDIC rooms, the operators scanned their screens for the submerged enemy craft. Hardly had the destroyers started to answer to their respective helms when they too witnessed the appalling destruction of the troopship. It sank about 100 miles NNW of Addu Attol, 00° 57′ north, 72° 16′ east.

* * *

The Japanese submarine, *I-27*, under the command of Captain Toshiaki Fukumura, had fired a salvo of four torpedoes, two narrowly missing the bows and the stern of the floundering ship. Only he and his crew would hear the unique sound, known to many submariners, of the screeching, metallic destruction ahead of them, eerily echoing through the hull of their own vessel, and indeed, reminding them of their own immediate peril. War was certainly no game for the faint-hearted.

Their attack on the *Khedive Ismail* was unusual. The Japanese commanders were under orders not to risk their boats, so they rarely attacked well-armed convoys, preferring isolated unarmed merchantmen. Possibly they had not noticed the full size of the convoy, or possibly their previous success in sinking no fewer than thirteen Allied ships under this same captain (making him Japan's top U-boat ace throughout the four-year conflict) had given them a false self-confidence (see the list of Allied ships sunk by *I-27*, in the Appendices).

* * *

HMS *Hawkins*, being the leader of the port column, had to take evasive action to avoid the fourth enemy warhead. Captain Josselyn recorded:

51

... The forecastle passed over the track of one torpedo which was already some distance away to port. The other torpedo was sighted on the starboard bow, running shallow and breaking surface. As *Hawkins* continued swinging to port, the torpedo was observed to have a yellow warhead and a brownish-red body. It eventually altered course, about 50° to starboard and disappeared. The first torpedo was running on an estimated track of 015° and the second 025°.

* * *

The *Khedive Ismail's* chief officer, John Duncan, said the following in a statement made and signed on the 21st February 1944:

... On 12th February 1944 at 09.03 GMT (14.33 local time), being asleep at the time, I was awakened by an explosion and immediately concluded that it could only be a torpedo hitting the ship. The vessel commenced listing to starboard at a speed which showed it was serious. Rushing along the boat deck, I found only the troop officer, Leleu. No one else was about – they had all cleared. The Troop Officer and myself then ran to the upper bridge. The Officer of the Watch, Quartermasters and lookouts had all left. I could not see the Commander, and as the vessel was at an angle of 40 degrees with the after end of the vessel sinking rapidly, I ordered the Troop Officer over the side and left myself.

Getting away from the vessel the foremast came down and missed me by about a foot, and the boilers blew out as there was an escape of steam through the funnel as the vessel disappeared rapidly stern first.

I then swam to where the wreckage was, and found thirty odd liferafts and about ten lifeboats. Eight of the boats were upside down, and two upright, but they got spread over an area of about 100 yards. Arriving at the rafts and upturned lifeboats, I got everyone in my vicinity into a comfortable position as I knew we would be picked up before long. The rafts held four people sitting and the the upturned lifeboats about twelve. One lifeboat, which was upright, I got baled out and had all the people who couldn't look after themselves put into it. I put the Troop Officer in charge of the lifeboat, and remained on the rafts with five Army officers and about twenty Africans, lashing the rafts end for end to keep them from being separated.

* * *

The 2nd officer, Cecil Munday, was interviewed shortly after the tragic incident. This is what he said:

... At the time of the attack the SS *Varsova*, leading the starboard column, was slightly ahead of station. No information regarding submarines operating in the vicinity was received, but during the forenoon of the 12th February the Master (Captain Whiteman) suggested to the captain of HMS

Hawkins that the convoy should commence zig-zagging, to which the captain replied that he would consider the matter and let the Master know his decision before nightfall.

[Author's note: this last statement is untrue. True, it was the Commodore who made the first signal on the morning of the 12th, at 07.45. But it read: 'If zig-zag was omitted and commenced at dawn tomorrow Sunday, we could save daylight on 14th. I estimate the speed overground from pm observed to am observed at 12.3 knots. What do you think?' Captain Josselyn replied at 08.54: 'Your 07.45. Yes I feel we cannot afford to zig-zag yet, though the One and a Half Degree Channel is an obvious haunt for a U-boat. Let us reconsider the matter at dawn tomorrow.' Out of common courtesy, a further message was sent, five minutes later, to the captain of HMS *Petard*; a humorous reply followed. See Appendices, for signals sent.] To continue:

... HM Destroyers *Petard* and *Paladin* were zig-zagging out on the wings during the morning, but at the time of the attack they were steering a steady course.

[Author's note: according to all the other reports the two escorting destroyers were still zig-zagging.]

Nothing of incident occurred until 14.40 on the 12th February, when in position 00° 57′ N - 72° 16′ E., steering N 85° E at 13 knots, we were struck almost simultaneously by two torpedoes. The weather was fine and sunny, with good visibility; there was a calm sea and light airs.

I am of the opinion the submarine fired a fan of torpedoes from the starboard quarter of the convoy; I was on watch at the time, talking to one of the signalmen, when I saw the wake of one torpedo pass our stern and miss the stern of HMS *Hawkins* by 50 feet. Immediately afterwards we were struck by a torpedo in No. 4 hold [Author's note: I have used Cliff Horrell's account. He said that the first torpedo struck in line with the third and fourth lifeboat. As he was stood on the stern of the SS *Varsova* at the time, I felt he had a better view to see where each warhead struck home] on the starboard side, followed five seconds later by a second torpedo, which struck in the boiler room, on the starboard side. No one saw the track of either of these torpedoes, but I sighted the U-boat's periscope about 400 feet away between the centre and starboard columns.

There was a loud explosion with the first torpedo, which caused the vessel to list 12 degrees to starboard; the second explosion, which was far more violent than the first, may have caused one of the boilers to explode. There was no flash with either explosion, but I saw flames rising outside the funnel, through the Fidley gratings. No water was thrown up, but a great amount of debris was flung high into the air. The second explosion caused the main stairway and troop deck to collapse, thereby trapping a great number of people. The vessel continued to heel over to starboard, until she was on her beam ends, and then disappeared.

Immediately after the second explosion, realising the serious position, I shouted 'every man for himself' and ran down to the bridge ladder. At the bottom of the ladder I saw the Captain, and on being told by him that the confidential papers were in their usual place, I went into his cabin, collected the bridge books and confidential papers, put them into a weighted bag and threw them overboard [he must have been extremely quick]. The wireless books were left in the wireless room and went down with the ship. On reporting to the Captain, he ordered me to abandon ship as nothing further could be done, adding that he himself would remain until everybody was clear. The ship finally sank 1 minute and 40 seconds after being torpedoed. There was no time to launch any boats, but many rafts and four lifeboats broke away as the ship sank. The Chief Officer and the Troop Officer ordered everybody to jump overboard as the ship was turning over. The Chief Officer jumped, but fouled some ropes and was pulled under with the ship; he eventually came to the surface, found a raft on to which he climbed and managed to pull onboard a Wren who was struggling in the water. He said that he felt no effect of suction on the low side of the ship as she sank. I went along to No. 2 boat and saw a Wren Officer lying on the deck; as she was unconscious and frothing at the mouth, I did not consider anything could be done for her, so I climbed over the high side and walked down the ship's side into the water.

I swam some half-dozen strokes from the ship when a big wave overtook me, and I was drawn under. I saw many bodies and wreckage floating past; I momentarily surfaced and managed to take a few deep breaths before being again drawn under. I was then on the port side of the ship, but on surfacing again I found myself off the starboard bow. I therefore must have passed completely under the ship. [Several eye-witnesses say that they saw the bow section poise upright and sink in a corkscrew fashion. This is probably what happened in this case.]

As I broke surface two natives, both wearing lifejackets, grabbed me, and, as I was not wearing my lifejacket, I literally had to fight them in order to keep myself afloat. I managed to shake them off, and swam amongst the wreckage for about half an hour before being pulled up to an upturned lifeboat by two sailors. There was a large bump on my head, evidently I had been hit by a piece of debris, and as I had swallowed a great quantity of water and fuel oil, I was violently sick for the next hour.

Most of the casualties occurred when the ship rolled over, many being killed whilst in the water by lifeboats which slid off the boat deck, and many others were killed when the troop deck and accommodation ladders collapsed. At the time of the incident many troops were in the saloon listening to a concert given by the Nursing Sisters; I learned later, from a man who was in this saloon and managed to escape through a porthole that, as the ship heeled over, the grand piano slid across the floor, pinning a number of people against the ship's side.

* * *

The 3rd radio officer, John Ainslie, was sunbathing on the boat deck at the time of the enemy attack. After instructing the two girls he was with to go to lifeboat stations, he assisted Captain Whiteman in clearing some of the other girls from the bathroom, whilst others inadvertently ran to their cabins to fetch forgotten life-jackets. He was finally instructed to leave the ship and was probably the last surviving person to see the captain alive, as he stood holding onto the handrail outside his accommodation. The 49-year-old skipper made no attempt to leave his ship. By this time, approximately 30 seconds had elapsed and, the ship was so far over that the officer was able to run down the port side of the troopship and dive into the water. He had only swum a couple of strokes when he turned over onto his back, just in time to see the bow section of the vessel turn completely over and disappear.

* * *

Gloria West was sitting on the starboard side of the promenade deck with her friend 'Tommy' Dunbar Thomson. An anonymous pianist was striking out the familiar chords of the Warsaw Concerto, which drifted from the concert taking place at the same level. Without any warning, there was an ear-splitting explosion. The music stopped abruptly, followed by an absolute silence before another, more violent, detonation threw her against the handrails. The stricken ship began to list heavily towards the sea. She hesitated against the rails, not knowing what to do, when a man appeared just a few feet away from her. She shouted, 'What shall I do?' He hastily replied, 'Jump!' Whereupon he launched himself from the side of the ship. She looked into the churning sea below, slipped the lifebelt over her unharnessed shoulder and shouted to her friend Tommy, who was still sat in the same position. With the sea about twenty-five feet below her and realising there were no other options open to her, she jumped. On reaching the turbulent water she swam away from the ship as quickly as she could; her progress was constantly hampered as she disentangled herself from ropes. Presumably these were attached to lifeboats which were, by

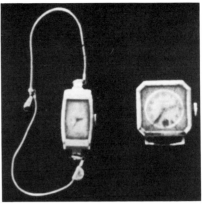

29 (left). Gloria West, who was the only survivor from the small contingent of the Women's Territorial Service.

30 (right). Photograph of the watches of Gloria West and Bill Power, both stopped at the time of the sinking of the *Khedive Ismail* – 2.35 pm.

now, at sea level but, lethally, still secured to the ship. Her persistence eventually bore fruit as she cleared the sinking wreckage. Her good friend Tommy did not survive. Neither did the other seven of her companions, all from the Women's Territorial Service (East Africa).

She swam away from the ship and then watched it turn upside down and disappear in a corkscrew fashion. Whilst treading water she heard the alarmed voice of Sergeant Bill Power who, while grasping his life-jacket, was announcing frantically that he could not swim. She found a sizable piece of wood which she pushed towards him, imparting renewed confidence. Inadvertently, they were slowly drifting away from the main bulk of the survivors, so she decided to tow the non-swimmer towards them. Their slow and energy-sapping progress was eventually accelerated with the assistance of Able Seaman John Smith, whilst distant cries for help drifted over the gentle undulation of the vast Indian Ocean.

* * *

Hubert Harwood, who was one of the Deck Officers onboard the SS *Ekma* at the time of the sinking, wrote his account in a letter he sent home to his wife and children in 1944:

> ... Having returned personnel, which included the band of the 4th Kings African Rifles, back to their headquarters in Dar-es-Salaam we went to Kilindini where we were to embark more troops for Ceylon. We spent about five days in Kilindini getting ready for the voyage. In addition to the four ships which had crossed from Ceylon: *Ekma, Khedive Ismail, Ellenga* and *Varsova* we found the *City of Paris* ready to join the convoy. We eventually set off from Kilindini, escorted by the cruiser *Hawkins* and three escort vessels *Landguard, Lulworth* and *Honesty.* When about fifty miles north of the Seychelles island group, the escort left and proceeded to Port Victoria. We had no further information regarding the six enemy submarines that had left Penang some weeks before and expected that there might possibly be some of them still at sea. The most likely place for them to be was somewhere near the Maldive Islands or between there and Ceylon.

> The *Khedive Ismail* had embarked eighty-four nurses and Wrens, otherwise the rest of the convoy contained East African troops. The voyage progressed without incident until we reached a point about 150 miles north-west of Addu Atoll, the southernmost part of the Maldive Islands. We were to go through the One and Half Degree Channel, which you will see marked on the map (unfortunately, the map has not survived the letter). We expected to see air escort that morning – it was Saturday – but none appeared. We were, however, joined by two Royal Navy escort ships *Paladin* and *Petard.* During the afternoon everyone was taking it easy, and aboard the *Khedive Ismail* there was a concert in the saloon. Personally, I was having a siesta. It was a beautiful afternoon, peaceful and calm. Suddenly at approximately 2.40 pm our alarm gongs clanged out all over the ship. Crew and troops ran hurriedly to their stations. I, first of all, rushed to the

bridge and reached it in about a minute from the time the gongs sounded. I didn't need to ask what had happened. A few yards ahead of us was a cloud of yellowish smoke and the *Khedive Ismail* had vanished beneath the waves. We were immediately astern of her at a distance of a little more than 500 yards, when the torpedoes struck and we had to alter course to avoid the wreckage and when we did pass through, all that was visible was two upturned lifeboats and two or three rafts and about fifty people in the water. I've never felt so helpless in my life. There were poor survivors in the water and amongst them a girl shouting 'help' and all we could do was to avoid the wreckage as much as possible and steam away from the scene at full speed. The *Khedive Ismail* was hit by two torpedoes simultaneously, broke in two and sank in 39 (thirty-nine) seconds.

* * *

In an account by Captain Denis Gun-Cuninghame, Master of SS *Ekma,* the incident was reported as follows:

... At 14.39 on 12th February 1944 (Zone time 5½) the *Khedive Ismail* suffered a violent explosion, was enveloped in a cloud of smoke and disappeared in 45 seconds (maximum). At the same time the 2nd Officer, Tregarthon Lovell, saw the track of one torpedo cross the bows of HMS *Hawkins.* I was sitting in my cabin when the attack took place and by the time I reached the bridge the *Khedive Ismail* had disappeared. All that remained was a cloud of yellow smoke slowly drifting away from the area of sinking. I saw that the helm was hard-a-port and ordered Lovell to take over the charge of the convoy and hoist flag 'I' for emergency turn to port. Both *Ekma* and *Hawkins* had turned to port on seeing the torpedoing and *Ekma* narrowly missed the *Khedive Ismail* which had, however, disappeared when *Ekma* came abreast of the position where she had been.

The starboard wing ships turned to starboard for avoiding action as *Varsova* had seen the periscope under her counter. HMS *Hawkins* is stated to have reported, by Aldis light, that two torpedoes had crossed her bows from starboard to port.

Ekma then took over the duties of the Commodore and *Hawkins* proceeded ahead to screen the convoy, which later reformed. *Ekma* states the torpedoes appeared to have passed astern of *Varsova,* one or more hitting the *Khedive Ismail* and one more passing ahead of *Hawkins.*

* * *

The Master of SS *Varsova,* Captain John Walton Knight, who was overwrought by the whole experience, said the following:

... I was on my bunk at the time and felt the *Varsova* shake from two explosions. Going quickly outside to the lower bridge deck, outside my cabin, I saw the *Khedive Ismail* heel over on her starboard side and, amid a large mound of smoke, disappear almost at once. Apparently, one torpedo struck under the bridge and the other in the boiler room. The convoy took avoiding action and I turned my ship to starboard. One torpedo could be seen crossing ahead of *Hawkins* (about 100 feet) and the torpedo gave no definite track but bursts of impulses on the water were observed and I thought it was travelling in jerks.

Only a few survivors could be seen, but I did see one boat with one man on top of it. The destroyers, which were stationed about six cables on either bow, turned outwards and steamed back towards the general area, where the transport had disappeared. I have lost faith in destroyers and their asdic. Furthermore, as no aircraft were present prior to the torpedoing, the subsequent constant air escort made me imagine that Japanese aircraft were about.

I am of the opinion that the U-boat sighted the convoy from ahead, passed deep on our opposite course under the starboard wing escort and came up after that (HMS *Petard*) had passed over. The U-boat raised its periscope close to *Varsova*'s stern, sighted and fired, and then dived deep, passing ahead of *Ellenga*.

* * *

V

ATTACK AT ALL COSTS

Before continuing with the story in this chapter it is necessary to explain the asdic methods deployed during the war by naval escort vessels.

The asdic beam was transmitted through the water by means of a cone installed in a retractable dome which was situated in the hull about one-third of the ship's length from the bows. When the sound wave struck an underwater object an echo bounced back to the receiver in the form of a 'ping' from which a skilful operator could determine both range and direction. By 'training on and off' the target it was possible to estimate the size and reliability of a genuine contact. However, it should be pointed out that the asdic beam could produce echoes not only from submarines, but also from the hulls of nearby ships, shoals of fish, disturbances in the water and even tide rips. Correct identification was only possible by an adept asdic team (usually comprising a control officer and first and second operators, the first operator taking over during action stations).

Another consideration was the Doppler effect, which caused the pitch of the echo to change and was dependent on whether the U-boat was moving away from (opening) or towards (closing) the transmitting ship, left or right. Again, this subtle complication could only be detected by the trained ear. If this was not enough to minimise any reasonable chance of success, some sea conditions created layers of water at differing temperatures which sometimes caused the asdic beam to bend or miss the target altogether.

The maximum operating speed was approximately 18 knots, as speeds above this masked and distorted the echoes. The ideal speed, when hunting a U-boat, was generally acknowledged to be 15 knots. When the attacking destroyer began its approach run it was quite normal to lose the echoes from about 300 yards; therefore, the only way to estimate the time for dropping the depth-charges was by the combination of both plotting table and stop watch. It was during this 'dead time' between losing contact and firing depth-charges, which did not descend with great speed, that the enemy had time to take evasive action.

The ideal team for attacking U-boats was two or even three ships, each striking in turn, and each maintaining a careful appraisal of the submarine's evasive movements and exchanging new information throughout the hunt. If a convoy was being attacked by a wolf-pack then it usually became impossible to spare more than one ship at a time, because of the immediate necessity to retain close escort.

The depth-charges could be set to explode at any depth between 50 and 500 feet and were filled with either 'Amatol' or 'Minol' explosives. Judging the depth was primitive and very difficult to estimate. Ideally, it was safer to drop depth-charges at high speed to reduce the chances of damage to the firing ship; unfortunately, as previously explained, this had the effect of disturbing asdic reception.

Locating and destroying the enemy submarine was the task now facing the convoy's destroyer escort.

* * *

As *Paladin* altered her course to 220°, steering the destroyer north of the position of the sunken troopship, her attacking course converged on the new route of the absconding cruiser *Hawkins* and the troopship *Ekma*, which were by now steering approximately 010°. Asdic contact was gained at 14.36 (09.06 GMT). Although this was later considered to have been wake from one of the spent torpedoes, a counter-attack was carried out with a ten-charge pattern of depth-charges which were dropped near the stern of the retiring cruiser. Meanwhile *Varsova* was flying No. 2 pennant (submarine to port). The combination of these two factors convinced Captain Gun-Cuninghame that the submarine attack had indeed come from the port side of the convoy, and so made an alteration of course to starboard. This change of direction was already being executed by *Hawkins* and was continued for a couple of minutes before *Ekma*'s other lookout stated that the attack had definitely come from the starboard side of the convoy, as he had seen the track of the periscope. Gun-Cuninghame put his ship back again to port. Captain Josselyn then signalled *Ekma* to 'Steam your fastest speed course 070°'. *Ekma* immediately complied, hoisting pennant K 14, indicating her new course. The *City of Paris* had already steered well out to port.

Contact was regained by *Paladin* six minutes later; this also proved to be a false reading, but a five-charge pattern was dropped nevertheless. At 14.45 the steamship *City of Paris* was rapidly closing the destroyer *Paladin* and, having resumed her former course (after an emergency turn to port), was seen to fire tracer off her port quarter at a suspected periscope. It was probably initiated by a trigger-happy gunner aiming at the curl of her own bow wave. *Paladin*'s course was therefore altered in the direction of fire and a single charge was dropped at 14.49. A fourth, and again unreliable, attack was executed eight minutes later with a pattern of ten depth-charges. At 14.51 an Aldis signal was sent by HMS *Hawkins*, in plain language. It was acknowledged four minutes later and read: 'Immediate. Join *Petard* and hunt. Rejoin convoy by dusk.'

The two destroyers were now about two miles apart, *Paladin* to the north and *Petard* almost due south of her. *Paladin* gained a final contact on her port quarter and Lieutenant Bailey, commander of the ship, quickly opened the range to 1000 yards and began his final approach. The attack was carried out on a firm contact moving left with moderate/high Doppler (the time taken for the echo to come back to the asdic operators, indicating a good contact). During the run in, wake was detected to the right of the target and a noise resembling the blowing of ballast tanks was reported by the operator. An accurate time of fire was obtained from the last inch of trace which was clearly defined and a nine-charge pattern dropped at 15.02 (09.32 GMT). This was considered by Bailey to be a reliable attack, asdic conditions being good, but unless there were two submarines, this seems unlikely.

At this stage, whilst a further pattern was being prepared and contact had been lost on the run out, *Paladin* began Operation 'Observant', heading westward. This manoeuvre was common practice when a contact had been lost and entailed 'boxing-in' the enemy: by the ships steaming in all four directions it was hoped to cover all the possible escape routes of the submarine.

Meanwhile *Petard*, in a similar period of time, had pursued her counter-attack further to the south. The commanding officer, Rupert Egan, believed he knew the approximate position of the submarine because the watch on his port bridge had also made a visual sighting of the periscope before the sinking. He purposely avoided dropping any depth-charges so as not to cause any disturbance which might jeopardise the asdic trace. Lieutenant K. Brooksbank, in charge of the asdic team, made a good contact at 14.48, about a mile south-west of the sinking. With doppler slight/high, at a range of 700 yards, this was confirmed as a submarine, but the counter-attack was delayed and the range opened up to 1,600 yards for a more positive attack with deep settings. Then, during the 14-knot approach, contact was lost and it became apparent that the enemy submarine had backtracked and was returning to the vicinity of the survivors (who were drifting slowly south-west due to the adverse set and the north-easterly, if moderate, wind). This tactical ploy was not uncommon. Egan sent a signal to *Paladin* at 15.00 which simply stated: 'Submarine is under survivors.'

With appalling implications, the enemy craft was now lying directly beneath a small number of the more scattered survivors. They were strung out amongst the outer fringes of flotsam, about 300 yards from the main concentration of boats, rafts and bobbing heads. Egan double-checked the operator's bearing and range, which only confirmed his fears. It was a *Catch-22* situation; before he could contemplate rescuing any of the survivors, he had to try to destroy the enemy. *Petard* scythed its way through the water, radiating a clean sparkling bow wave as it homed in on its prey. The scattered swimmers, fully expecting they were about to be picked up, waved and shouted as the warship closed on their area. It was not until the ship was right upon them that they realised the grim reality of the situation. Hope turned into horror as the first pattern was dropped. The seven charges (set at 230 feet) were fired from the port and starboard throwers and central trap at 15.00 (the same time that the signal was sent by Aldis lamp to *Paladin*). They splashed almost innocently into the sea, leaving the few survivors, nearby, frantically swimming to distance themselves from the ear-splitting explosion that would follow. The seconds agonisingly ticked by, as the 400 lb high-explosive canisters decended upon the submarine. Then, the surface of the sea shimmered and erupted into an enormous column of white water. The detonations reverberated like a heavy hammer-blow against the thin shell of the destroyer, underlining the awful consequences befallen by those straddled by the lethal charges and still in the water. The U-boat appeared to be pushed down as the movement recorded on asdic was slight.

Petard moved away before beginning a second attack. Black oil-ridden shapes floated in the path of the attack, as the enemy submarine dived even deeper. The eight charges (set at 300 feet) were launched at 15.05 and exploded with similar effect.

* * *

At this point in time, Buster (Percival Crabb) was still hanging onto the smoke float and remembered the almighty thump in the stomach as the depth-charges exploded below. He distinctly remembered one charge exploding, prematurely, on the surface. Other survivors later told him that these attacks nearly shook them off their rafts and the upturned lifeboat.

* * *

63

PASSAGE TO DESTINY

Dan Docwra continues his story:

> ... People were frantically trying to get themselves clear of the water as the depth charging commenced. The overcrowded lifeboat rocked from the nearby explosions. When the depth charges went off; if you were facing them it felt as if you had been hit by a train, the same if you had your back to them, it felt like a kick in the spine. The worst thing that I remember was this young coloured lad pleading to get onto the upturned lifeboat. One of the women pulled him by his arm and I pushed from below and then we saw that he was split complete from the left shoulder to the right hip and his stomach was just plopping out. She mimed 'let him go'. We had to let him slide back in the water and watch him drown. HMS *Paladin* sent out a motor boat to tell us the submarine was underneath us and he had to get us out of the way. He towed most of us out of the way then the *Paladin* came in and picked us up.

* * *

Brooksbank's asdic team again read the submarine on a clear signal and a third, and final, attack with depth charges, again with deep settings (300 feet), was launched at 15.13. Again, the pattern of nine charges fell in amongst a small contingent of survivors. They were now spread out over an area of about one square mile, with the majority concentrated in one sector. A further sweep only confirmed that contact had finally been lost. Before *Paladin* could complete 'Observant' Egan sent the following message at 15.19: 'Are you in contact?' Bailey replied two minutes later: 'Reply no. Suspect submarine to be one mile on my starboard beam.' He reinforced the signal four minutes later with: 'Am returning to scene now.' Only when Bailey signalled that he had lost contact at 15.30 did Egan request him to join him a minute later.

At 15.35 Bailey sent a signal that was to initiate the survivors welcomed rescue. It read: 'Shall I drop whaler with doctor to pick up survivors?' Egan gave permission a minute later and for the next three-quarters-of-an-hour the rescue proceeded.

Although it is almost certain that some of the swimmers were killed by Egan's offensive against the submarine, it must be remembered that many more would have been killed if the enemy had managed to fire another torpedo on a ship of the convoy. It could also be argued, although it was not the result of a conscious policy, that the constant detonations, which continued for approximately forty minutes, almost certainly saved some of the survivors from being attacked by sharks.

While *Paladin* was lowering her boats a great deal of air broke the surface close to the south-west of the wreckage and about 1,000 yards east of *Petard*. As no submarine contact was obtained throughout the rescue, it was thought to be air escaping from the wreck of the sunken troopship.

* * *

Eddie Turner continues his story as he clung to the side ropes of the carley float:

> ... I then noticed one of the destroyers had turned and was coming in our direction depth charging, so I held my legs out of the water as best I could through fear of the depth charging and also sharks (even though I never saw any). I drifted towards a lifeboat where I thought I would be better off and climbed aboard. They were still depth charging. Apparently the submarine was hiding below the wreckage and the survivors. In the lifeboat were two females, I think one was a Wren who said that she had crawled through a porthole, also a Leading Seaman called White who said it was the third time that he had been torpedoed. There was also a Sub-Lieutenant and a Swahili soldier who was in a bad way; there seemed to be sort of soap bubbles coming out of his mouth. I noticed several bodies floating about, one I noticed was an Army officer, by the pips on his shoulder, who I think had been hit by depth charges, judging by his mauve and bruised face.

* * *

Cecil Munday's account continues:

> ... We hung onto to this upturned lifeboat for about one-and-a-half hours, during which time the destroyers *Paladin* and *Petard* were dropping depth charges, which shook the lifeboat so much that we had difficulty in maintaining our hold. Eventually both destroyers lowered their motor launches and picked up survivors, most of whom were taken on board HMS *Paladin*.

* * *

William Thomson also witnessed the two destroyers cruising about, dropping depth-charges dangerously close to them. After about an hour, one of the destroyers started picking up the survivors. Within about an hour-and-a-half after the transport had sunk, most of them were safely on board.

* * *

Captain John Walton Knight, of the *Varsova,* stated at the Board of Enquiry:

> ... The depth-charge explosions lifted survivors bodily and may have injured or killed some of them.

As the *Varsova* was steaming away from the scene at the time, he must have observed this through binoculars because, by the time that the destroyer *Petard* had dropped the first pattern at 15.00 (09.30 GMT) she would have been nearly seven miles away, hardly a credible distance to make such an accurate observation.

* * *

Captain Denis Gun-Cuninghame, of SS *Ekma,* similarly states in his report:

> ... The two destroyers reversed course and came down their respective sides of the convoy, dropping depth charges lavishly at frequent intervals, The port wing destroyer hoisted the cone and red flag [signal for U-boat contact] when turned and attacking with depth charges, The attacks continued until the convoy had passed almost out of sight of the destroyers.

After the initial turn to port both *Hawkins* and *Ekma* turned back to starboard as the port wing destroyer (stated to be *Paladin*) passed very close to the stern of *Hawkins* on an opposite course and dropping depth charges.

The depth charge attack amongst some of the survivors was such a graphic incident that it inspired part of Nicholas Montserrat's famous novel *The Cruel Sea* ('Part Three, 1941: Grappling, Section 7').

* * *

Buster, along with several other survivors, was eventually picked up from an upturned lifeboat (to which he had swum after the depth-charging) and taken to *Paladin.* As he reached the top of the scrambling net he was given a pair of sandals by one of the crew, who informed him that they were to protect his bare feet from the scorching hot deck. During the period he was in the sea, his plaster cast had dissolved and fallen away from his recovering leg. It seemed to cause him little trouble as he was able to put some weight on it, even though the muscles had naturally wasted. He looked at some of the survivors around him and can distinctly recall one of the Wrens boasting two black eyes. She had evidently been struck, on the bridge of her nose and forehead, by a sizable piece of surface-bound debris.

* * *

Lieutenant-Colonel Stevens went on to describe their eventual rescue:

> ... When we had been in the boat for about an hour, *Paladin* picked us up while *Petard* stood by. None of the survivors was badly hurt and we scrambled aboard to be received by the matelots with cigarettes and mugs of tea. Those of us who hadn't our shoes found we could not walk on the iron deck. It was as hot as a grill.

* * *

Meanwhile, *Petard* carried out a sweep to the westward, but failed to regain contact and returned half-an-hour later to lower a motorboat and whaler to assist with the search. Whilst she momentarily remained stationary, her crew picked up just over a dozen survivors and two dead Wrens.

31. Japanese submarine *I-27* breaks the surface astern of HMS *Paladin*.

Another large air bubble broke the surface, nearby, north-west of the wreckage. A search was therefore carried out on a course of 312°, but asdic contact was not obtained, but unexpectedly, at 16.20 (10.50 GMT), amidst a rapturous roar of applause from survivors and the ship's companies of both *Paladin* and *Petard* the U-boat surfaced in a voluminous mass of blown compressed air and spray, about one-and-a-half miles off their starboard quarter. It was motionless.

67

32. Closer view of the large Japanese submarine clearly showing the large gun positioned in front of the conning tower.

At this instant, *Paladin* had almost completed the recovery and quickly hoisted up her scrambling nets to prevent them fouling the propellers. Only one whaler from *Paladin,* a whaler and a motor cutter from *Petard* and an upright lifeboat from *Khedive Ismail* remained prominently visible in the water.

Both ships turned in unison to attack the large U-boat, which was initially identified as a type B1 scouting submarine, known to be just over 350 feet long and displacing over 2,500 tons (surfaced). It had a black painted hull and a grey casing and was almost the same length and tonnage as the two 'P' Class destroyers that had hunted it to the surface. Both ships opened fire simultaneously, with all trainable guns, scoring many hits. *Petard* then passed as close to the stern of the stationary vessel as practicable and fired three depth-charges from her port throwers and trap (set to 50 feet). They all fell reasonably close, but caused no visible damage.

33. HMS *Paladin* moving in to ram *I-27*, photographed from HMS *Petard.*

Suddenly the Japanese U-boat, *I-27*, started moving, steering approximately 250° at around 4 knots. She quickly squared off her trim and appeared to be under control. As nobody immediately ventured onto the conning tower and the bow started to dip, Lieutenant Bailey surmised that the U-boat had surfaced due to an error in trim and was about to re-submerge. He therefore decided that the only course of action was to ram the vessel and signalled his intentions to *Petard* at 16.21. As the destroyer raced towards the enemy, Bailey reduced speed to 20 knots and opened fire with the four-inch guns, scoring at least one hit on the submarine's rounded hull until it became impossible to depress the guns enough to hit the target. All the crew and survivors were told to lie flat on the deck or hang onto something solid in readiness for the expected collision. Four minutes later, when she was about 600 feet from the U-boat, Egan signalled: 'Do not ram.' Bailey acted on this order but still considered it essential to place depth charges under the U-boat to prevent it from diving.

34. HMS *Paladin*. She nearly sank when she collided with the Japanese submarine.

As the bow swung to port, the ship listed, enabling the four-inch pom poms and oerlikons to bear. They all opened fire in unison as he shouted the necessary steering and engine movements to flip across the enemy's bow. Unfortunately, the cumulative noise from the guns was so loud that the coxswain was unable to hear Bailey's command, 'Stop port, full ahead port, starboard 30.' The Lieutenant, therefore, had to kneel down, thrust his head and shoulders through the wheelhouse hatch and scream into the ear of the coxswain. The result of this untimely delay, at such a crucial moment, was that, although the destroyer's swing was checked before striking the U-boat, the forward hydroplane entered the ship's starboard side, tearing an 80-foot gash 12 inches below the waterline. This caused extensive flooding in the engine room, gearing room, Numbers 5 and 7 fuel tanks and the after magazine. There was an air pressure showing on No. 8 fuel tank sounding tube, possibly due to a previously suspected leak from No. 7 tank. The nature of the damage indicated that the hydroplanes of the submarine had probably been in the dive position.

ATTACK AT ALL COSTS

As the stern of *Paladin* passed the U-boat, two further depth charges were fired, one of which exploded right under the enemy's bows. It is considered that this charge, coupled with the damage to her port hydroplane during the collision, probably prevented the U-boat from diving and escaping.

Two minutes later, five men appeared in the conning tower and moved quickly down the vertical ladder, striving to man the large 5½-inch gun which was mounted forward of the bridge on the main deck. At this point *Paladin* was lying 400 yards away on the enemy's port bow. The No. 2 oerlikon gunner quickly dealt with the situation when he opened fire at close range. One man fell overboard, dead, whilst two more were killed where they stood. Understandably, the other two beat a hasty retreat before they too suffered a similar fate. From this moment on, the stationary *Paladin* only took an intermittent part in the combat, as and when range and direction allowed.

* * *

Eddie Turner continues his story, still in the lifeboat:

> ... The submarine then surfaced about 50 yards away from us and seemed to be damaged as it was going round in circles. One of the destroyers was coming in to ram the submarine and turned off rather late. The submarine's bows caught her starboard aft and apparently damaged her rudder and starboard propeller. We drifted in the lifeboat towards the damaged destroyer *Paladin*. They had thrown scambling nets over the side on which we climbed up and got aboard. I was helped onto the deck by a Chief Petty Officer in immaculate white overalls. He said, 'Blimey, they're sending kids out here now' and asked me if I wanted to go to the sickbay. I said 'No'. At that time they piped 'Lighten ship'. I was on the stern near the 4.7-inch gun which they were firing but could not depress low enough. I started throwing empty shell cases over the side. Meanwhile a seaman was firing the oerlikon gun at the submarine and I could hear the crashes hitting the conning tower. I believe the Japanese were trying to reach their deck gun.

* * *

A running action now ensued which lasted for nearly an hour, during which time the enemy submarine circled blindly, creating an uncomfortable and significant threat to both ships. Her periscopes had been bent during the previous encounter, when *Paladin*'s starboard motor cutter (which was in the process of being stowed) had smashed into the vessel's 'eyes', rendering it blind to any surface action (unless a direct peep was made through any of the holes created by the Allied gunnery on the casing of the conning tower). The submarine was down by the stern and,

71

using her diesel engines, varied her speed from six to ten knots. Over three hundred rounds of four-inch ammunition were expended (unfortunately only 40 were semi-armour-piercing, as no more were available prior to sailing from Trincomalee). There were a high percentage of hits which had riddled the conning tower and blown away her large gun but this had still failed to halt her in any way. The barrage of fire was not only intended to help sink the submarine, but also to prevent its crew from taking stock of the stationary state of *Paladin*. The U-boat was certainly capable of ramming her, and might even have been able to fire torpedoes.

Tackling a U-boat which was on the surface and still moving was an intractable problem. Ordinary gunfire inflicted no apparent damage to the pressure hull and lobbing depth-charges at it would involve getting precariously close. Only semi-armour-piercing shells would have much chance of success, and these were already expended. (The SHARK anti-submarine projectile had recently been developed for use in 4-inch guns, explicitly for use against U-boats on the surface. Shark was a camouflage name; its official name was 'projectile, 4-inch, anti-submarine'. It was designed for close-range use and was aimed just short of the U-boat and struck the boat underwater where the water tamping would make its detonation more effective. Unfortunately, at this time the new weapon was not available in the Eastern waters.) Another option was to board the submarine to plant detonating devices directly on her hull, but it was not possible to get close enough to board safely, and there was every chance that the Japanese, sensing what was happening, would blow themselves up along with their conquerors.

With *Paladin* stationary and with most of *Khedive Ismail*'s survivors now aboard her, it was imperative to find a speedy conclusion. Egan therefore decided to try to sink the U-boat by torpedo. The textbook procedure, prescribed by the torpedo school at HMS *Vernon*, was to position one's ship on a parallel course to the enemy, checking the speed and distance, and, as soon as the first of at least a salvo of three or four torpedoes was despatched, to turn the ship away from the target and fire the remainder, creating a lethal spread of fire with a greater chance of scoring a hit.

However, possibly disturbed by the unnerving decision to depth-charge amongst some of his own countrymen, the fact that *Paladin* was in danger of sinking and that the large submarine was virtually a sitting duck, Rupert Egan decided against this drill. He was no doubt also aware of the large cost of the torpedoes (£1,200 each) and their limited supply, and had not unreasonable confidence in his torpedo officer, Robert de Pass. He ordered the firing of single torpedoes at the target.

35. The anti-submarine destroyer HMS *Petard*.
She had joined the Eastern Fleet in January 1943.

The first 'tin fish' was sent towards the *I-27* at 17.00 and, travelling at approximately 40 knots, should have reached its quarry within a minute. After two minutes had elapsed, it became apparent that it had missed. Ten minutes later a second torpedo was dispatched; once again, to no avail.

Two more were fired, singly, all reaching a similar conclusion, exhausting the supply of the forward quadruple torpedo mounting. Apprehension and disappointment filled the ship. If all the precious torpedoes were wasted, the submarine would have to be boarded in a possibly suicidal mission. Gunner Leuillete, supervising the forward mounting, was so frustrated by the loss of his missiles that he shouted at the Bridge, demanding that he be allowed to take over the control of the last few torpedoes. It is unlikely that Egan heard his mutinous protest; but the whole ship remained extremely tense at the failure. The second supply was engaged from the rear mounting.

Desperately, the fifth and sixth torpedoes were fired to no avail, and the submarine, possibly now aware of what was happening, now seemed to be attempting evasive manoeuvres. Morale was at an all-time low when the seventh torpedo left the tube, but at 17.23 (11.53 GMT), the seventh struck

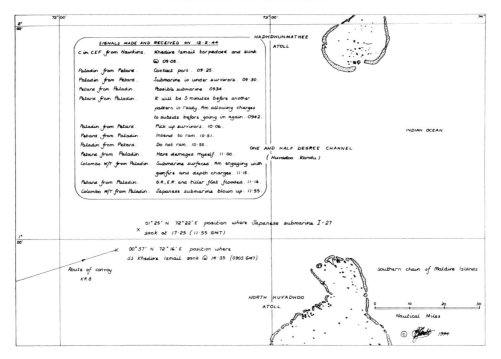

36. Plan showing the estimated positions of the sinking of the *Khedive Ismail* and the Japanese submarine *I-27* in relation to the One and a Half Degree Channel.

home, blowing the submarine in half with a huge column of water and flame. As the explosion subsided, the bows and the stern raised skywards, like two steel headstones, marking her deathly passage to the deep and quiet waters that had claimed her own prey three hours earlier. Such was the mood on the ship, there were hardly any cheers as the hit was scored. A wireless transmission was sent to Colombo two minutes later. It simply stated 'Japanese submarine blown up.'

The submarine that had claimed fourteen Allied ships, totalling 82,979 tons since her present captain had taken command in early 1943, had finally disappeared. *Petard* closed the area but there were no survivors; only a growing patch of diesel oil and few pieces of wood marked her grave. There are several 'Most Secret' messages preserved in Admiralty files which purport to record the survival of one of the Japanese crew but no further evidence has confirmed these reports, and survival seems unlikely.

Petard returned to pick up the whaler belonging to *Paladin* and her own whaler and motor cutter. They contained some of the ship's crew and the remaining survivors from the sunken transport. All that remained were

74

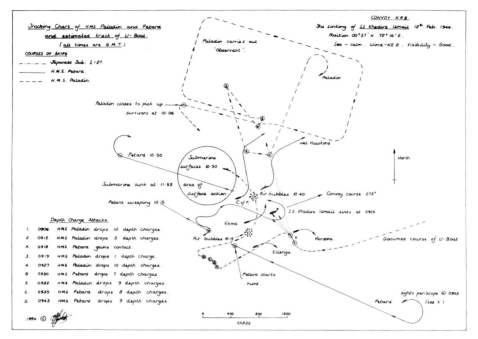

37. Tracking chart of HM Ships *Paladin* and *Petard* and the estimated track of *I-27*.

the still forms of corpses, either floating face down, and anonymous, or bobbing about in the oil-ridden swell, supported by their lifejackets. Seven minutes after the huge submarine had started its descent to the ocean bed, another violent underwater explosion occurred, which only brought more diesel oil and debris to the surface, samples of which were recovered.

During *Petard*'s triumphant action, *Paladin* had been fighting desperately to stay afloat. The collision had caused a 20° list to starboard and her after, main deck was nearly awash. The engineering officer, Lieutenant Commander (E) Bowman, had managed to organise his department into effective groups. In turn, they had managed to shore up the gash with temporary seals made from hammocks, transfer fuel to other parts of the ship and discharge most of the unwanted sea-water. The latter was achieved when a stand-by diesel-driven dynamo was put on-line, enabling the pumps (those that were not below water) to be used to good effect. The list had been reduced by about 5°. Meanwhile, the torpedoes had been launched and the aftermost ammunition moved to the port of the ship along with all the able-bodied survivors. Bailey defends this decision to expend all his remaining torpedoes by saying in his report that this

38. Some of the survivors on board HMS *Petard.*

expensive course of action possibly saved the ship at a critical moment
before pumps became effective.

Bailey now reported that he was in danger of sinking as he had very
little buoyancy aft and there was a possibility of the forward engine room
bulkhead not holding. Meanwhile, Egan had returned from picking up the
motor boat and whaler, and went alongside *Paladin* to embark all the
rescued and relieve him of some of his Ship's Company. A tow was then
passed and course shaped 160° for Addu Atoll. It began shortly after sunset.

Meanwhile, the awful task of preparing the two dead Wrens for burial
was supervised by the Chief Bo'sun's Mate who was obviously disturbed by
his necessary duties. The off-watch crew and some of the survivors
assembled on the quarter deck whilst the two inert, weighted canvas bags
lay before them. Lieutenant Commander Egan read out a short service and
the bodies were individually slid down greased boards, under a white
ensign and commended to the deep. The sombre and poignant interment

of just two of the victims (the rest had inevitably been left in the sea) left no one unaffected by the grim realities of war. It was, during a conflict that mainly involved men, considered especially tragic to lose women, especially so many women who were not only young, but who had been trained as nurses to save lives.

* * *

Douglas Freer, an Ordinary Seaman aboard *Petard,* recalls the emotional state of some of the East African survivors, who were accommodated in his mess, after the rescue:

> They were utterly bewildered by the whole episode. Many were experiencing their first trip at sea and most of them had probably never even heard of submarines. An example of the vast cultural difference between the British and East African forces was highlighted when one of the messmen made them cups of tea and offered them milk and sugar. An English warrant officer intervened, believing that if the Africans got used to such luxuries, they would not be able to cope later on when there would be none available. [Such bizarre behaviour would be unthinkable today.] They were all completely lost in the situation.

* * *

HMS *Petard* continued the tow, at a speed of 8 knots, and covered the 100-mile journey to Addu Atoll without further incident athough the tow parted during the morning of the 13th. This happened when negotiating the fairway buoys on entering the atoll. By a combination of good fortune and seamanship, Egan got a new line on board and regained control, before *Paladin* floundered on the reef. They eventually berthed alongside the oiler *British Loyalty.*

During the voyage to the safe haven of Addu Atoll officers on board *Petard* recorded the names of all the fortunate survivors. It was only then that the scale of the disaster became apparent. The doctor on *Petard,* Lieutenant Finbar Prendergast, and his assistants worked through the night attending to the survivors, giving first aid and cleaning the oil off their skins.

* * *

This was the third largest merchant sea tragedy during the Second World War, and the occasion of the largest loss of Allied servicewomen in a single incident. (The worst merchant incident was the loss of the *Lancastria* in 1940; the second worst was the loss of the *Laconia* in 1942.)

The crew of *Khedive Ismail,* including officers, totalled 178; only 6 officers and 16 crew members were rescued. Captain R. C. Whiteman, DSC, who could possibly have saved himself, seemingly chose to go down with his ship.

There was one matron and 53 nursing sisters who were intended to staff the 150th General Hospital at Colombo, destined to be the base hospital for the 11th East African Division. Only 3 sisters survived, Phyllis Hutchinson being one of them.

Of the 19 members of the Women's Royal Naval Service on board, only two survived, Norah Munro being one of them.

Lieutenant Commander, Leslie Merrill, RN, and his civilian wife and baby son also perished. A War Correspondent named Kenneth Gandar Dower also lost his life.

Gloria West, who was a lance corporal in the Women's Territorial Service, was the sole survivor from nine members of this branch of the Army on the ship.

In all, only six of the 83 women on board were rescued.

From 252 Royal Naval personnel who were on board, only 43 survived. There were 11 DEMS (an acronym for Defensively Equipped Merchant Ships, a British organisation set up to provide guns and gun crews for merchant ships) on board, consisting of 4 gunners from the Royal Maritime Artillery and 7 men from the Royal Navy (their numbers are included in the previous totals). Their sole purpose was to maintain and operate the troopship's guns. All were lost.

From the 996 Army personnel, both black and white, forming the 301st Field Regiment, only 143 survived.

In short, of the 'official' 1,511 complement on board the *Khedive Ismail*, only 214 survivors were recovered. Unbelievably, 1,297 had perished (see the lists of both casualties and survivors in the Appendices).

* * *

For their action during the difficult destruction of the large Japanese submarine, four members of HMS *Petard* were mentioned in despatches by Commander Rupert C. Egan. They were: Temporary Lieutenant K. Brooksbank, who controlled the ASDIC department and Able Seaman K. V. Lacroix, who operated the same equipment. Similar credit was also given to Temporary Lieutenant Gordon G. Connell, who commanded the gun crews. The last named wrote a history of HMS *Petard* (*Fighting Destroyer*, published in 1976), but this appeared before access to many crucial Admiralty documents, such as the report of the Board of Enquiry, was possible. The fourth acknowledgment was given to Leading Seaman A. J. Hopkins, for his skill and resourcefulness as Captain of X gun.

HMS *Hawkins* arrived at Addu Atoll at 17.30 on the same day (13th). However, it was not until the following morning that *Petard* moored alongside the old cruiser and all the survivors were transferred into the more spacious accommodation that the larger ship provided. In the evening, the damaged *Paladin* came alongside to acquire more pumps and collision mats required for the next stage of her journey.

Just before noon, on the 15th February, *Hawkins* weighed anchor and set sail for her original destination (zig-zagging all the way); she was played away by Lieutenant-Colonel Lea's 26th/15th Punjab Regiment's pipe band, who circled the ship in a landing craft. Forty-eight hours later, she passed the breakwater at Colombo. As the ship approached the quay-side it was eagerly awaited by dozens of Australian Red Cross ambulances ready to transport all the survivors for both treatment and precautionary check-ups. The following day, Buster was taken to the shore establishment HMS *Lanka* where he received further checks before beginning a week's survival leave.

After the requisite health inspections by the hospital staff, during which time the Africans were delighted to receive an issue of pyjamas, the remnants of the 301st Field Regiment were reunited with the score or so of officers who had been on another ship.

One interesting fact brought about by the sinking of the Japanese submarine *I-27*, although helped by *Paladin* in the earlier part of the action, was that *Petard* became the only British warship to sink a U-boat from all three countries at war with Britain during the Second World War.

The German *U-559* had been sunk by her in October 1942. This had been accomplished with the help of another destroyer after an epic fourteen-hour hunt. Lieutenant Anthony Fasson, of *Petard*, swam out to the rapidly sinking U-boat closely followed by Able Seaman Colin Grazier. They succeeded in salvaging vital decoding material but, unfortunately, went down with the stricken vessel. Their great act of bravery undoubtedly helped to reduce some of the losses endured in the Battle of the Atlantic. This enabled the cypher breakers at Bletchley to forewarn the Admiralty of impending U-boat movements, due to the current code books that were captured at this time. They were both posthumously awarded the George Cross. The one survivor of the boarding party, 16- year-old Canteen Assistant Tommy Brown, became the youngest recipient of the George Medal.

Six weeks later, along with the Greek destroyer *Queen Olga*, *Petard* depth-charged the Italian U-boat *Uarsciek* to the surface after its failure to torpedo the two Allied ships. *Petard* tried to tow the 'prize' into Malta but, when it became apparent that the submarine was sinking, *Petard*'s boarding and towing party removed all the Italian charts and signal books. These, too, revealed valuable and detailed information as to the whereabouts of enemy minefields in the Sicilian narrows and beach defences. They were to prove priceless for the planners of the final push into North Africa and the subsequent landings in Sicily.

In contrast, HMS *Paladin* had sunk *U-205* in February 1943, off the North African port of Derna, also capturing valuable coding equipment.

The mood of the time is reflected in the outspoken 'Special Order' issued by Major General C. C. Fowkes, Commander of the 11th (East African) Division which had lost so many men, on 15th February:

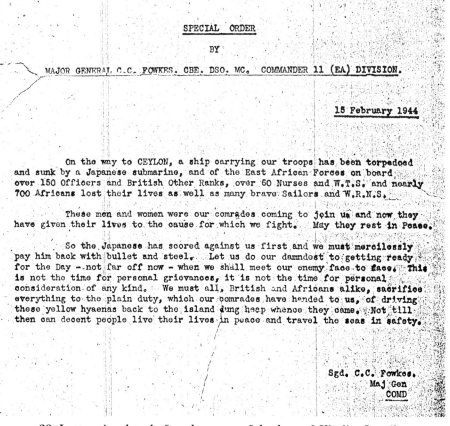

39. Letter circulated after the news of the loss of *Khedive Ismail.*

As with all merchant losses, even those incurred in war, a Board of Enquiry was set up to report on the sinking of the *Khedive Ismail.*

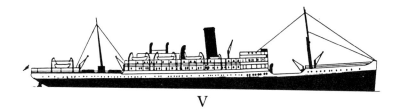

V

THE BOARD OF ENQUIRY

Under the explicit direction of Admiral Sir James Somerville, who was the Commander-in-Chief of the Eastern Fleet at the time of the tragic incident, a memorandum was sent, on 15th February 1944, to HMS *Lanka*, a shore establishment in Colombo, Ceylon. It was addressed to Rear Admiral R. S. G. Nicholson, DSO, DSC, Captain C. A. Merriman, RN (Retired) and Lieutenant Commander C. W. North, RN. In it were a clear set of instructions delegating Rear Admiral Nicholson as president of the proceedings. They were to hold a full and careful investigation into the circumstances attending the sinking of the SS *Khedive Ismail* on 12th February 1944 whilst in convoy, calling before them such witnesses as were necessary to enable them to form a correct conclusion. Enclosed with the memorandum were the narratives of events obtained from the captains of SS *Varsova* and SS *Ekma*, together with rough diagrams depicting the position of the ships in convoy KR8. These were to be augmented by reports from the Commanding Officers of ships of the escort, which would be sent later. The enquiry was to consider the following questions:

(a) The number of escorts employed and whether in the circumstances prevailing at the time these could, or should, have been increased.

(b) Whether air escort was available and, if so, whether it was employed to the best advantage.

(c) The anti-submarine (shown as A/S hereafter) tactics and dispositions employed by the convoy and its escort.

(d) Whether the construction or condition of the *Khedive Ismail* in any way contributed to the rapid sinking of the vessel.

(e) Whether there were any grounds to suggest that the sailing and route of the convoy might have been known to the enemy.

The necessary authorities had already been informed and directed to afford the board all the necessary facilities.

The Board of Enquiry was convened for 16th and 17th February 1944, almost immediately, and was held in the Flag Officer's office, Naval Office II, at HMS *Lanka*. The small Spartan room was panelled half way up the walls with varnished oak planking whilst the upper walls and ceiling were distempered white. A few large oil paintings, depicting naval heroes of the past, were hung in the centres of each wall. Beside the wooden entrance door hung a framed coloured copy of a painting of King George VI. In the centre of the room was a horseshoe-shaped table with three solid walnut chairs spaced around its perimeter. To the left of the table was a small office table with a typewriter and another chair, of more basic design, neatly placed in front of it. The high ceiling, marbled floor and lack of general comfort created a cold and imposing atmosphere – perfect for such an investigation. (Many of the minor details in this account were clearly remembered by Cliff Horrell and related to the author.)

On Wednesday morning, 16th February, the enquiry began with Captain Herbert Percival, master of SS *City of Paris*. He was shown into the room by a smartly dressed marine who saluted the board and then retired outside, closing the door quietly behind him. The captain was asked to stand in the middle of the open-ended table and face Rear Admiral Nicholson who was seated in the centre. In front of him were a small pile of papers, a large blotting pad, an ink pot and dark-blue fountain pen. To the captain's right was Lieutenant Commander North and to his left was Captain Merriman. Behind him sat a smartly dressed Wren, complete with pencil and pad ready to record his answers in shorthand.

The Rear Admiral began his cross-examination by asking him his name and whether his ship was present at the time of the submarine attack on 12th February 1944. He was then asked various questions concerning the incident.

The second person to be interrogated was Commander Arthur Guy Denis Bagot who was the Naval Control Service Officer at Colombo. His line of questioning concerned the standing orders which govern the zig-zagging procedures of a convoy, the person responsible for deciding the zig-zag policy and, after the conferences preceding a convoy, the person who gives the ruling after the discussion. It was explained, by Commander Bagot, that ships with a speed of 11 knots or over are to zig-zag, when in company, as laid down in Convoy Instructions, but that the penultimate ruling is given by the Naval Control Service Officer after careful discussion with the Commodore and with the Senior Officer of the Escort in attendance. The final decision would normally be recorded on a questionnaire sheet presented at the pre-sailing conference.

He went on to explain the procedures at Colombo, stating that the questionnaire would be shown to each Master. Any subsequent alteration was the responsibility of the Commodore with the concurrence of the Senior Officer of the Escort. Once at sea further considerations, on that decision, were explicitly that of the Commodore unless he was overruled by the Senior Officer of the Escort for operational purposes. ETA (Expected Time of Arrival) was calculated by the Naval Control Service Officer, allowing for zig-zag or lack of zig-zag, at the conference.

Already, it can be seen that the line of questioning was primarily concerned with the absence of zig-zag. Had the convoy reached its destination safely without zig-zag then the omission of the manoeuvre would presumably have been acceptable.

The witness withdrew and Captain Percival, Master of the *City of Paris*, was recalled. Straight away, the line of questioning homed in on what Commander Bagot had previously clarified. When asked about the conference at Kilindini, the captain revealed that no questionnaire concerning the movements of the forthcoming convoy KR8 had been distributed, only one for equipment and the like. However, he did say that the issue concerning the zig-zag of the convoy had most definitely been discussed. He stressed Captain Whiteman's opposition to the manoeuvre, whilst Captain Josselyn had been clearly in favour.

Next to be interviewed, separately, were the 2nd Officer Tregarthon Lovell and Cadet Norman Smith, both from the *City of Paris*. They had together been on the 12 to 4 watch at the time of the sinking. Their line of interrogation only concerned what they saw, the cadet being the first to observe the periscope from the bridge of their ship, close to the stern of the *Varsova*. They briefly described the rapidity of the sinking of the *Khedive Ismail*.

Captain Denis Gun-Cuninghame, Master of the *Ekma*, was then summoned to the room. When asked to explain to the Board, in his own words, what he actually saw, he more or less reiterated what he had already said in his interview with Captain Thelwell, which had been handwritten and produced to the board before the enquiry had begun. The questioning then briefly touched on the construction of the *Khedive Ismail* and whether he considered that a more modern ship would have taken longer to sink. He was also asked about the depth-charging and confirmed that the first attack, by HMS *Paladin*, took place nearly a mile away from the survivors.

As with Captain Percival, Captain Gun-Cuninghame was queried about the conference at Kilindini with regard to the decision to zig-zag and who had made the final decision on the zig-zag policy for the convoy. He was most definite with his answer, stating that Captain Josselyn, of *Hawkins*, was responsible for that judgment whilst the Commodore merely implemented its execution. He was then asked if it was not the case that rules were laid down as to whether to zig-zag or not. Gun-Cuninghame's reply was that there were no definite rules laid down as to a convoy's speed or the inclusion or exclusion of zig-zag manoeuvres throughout a voyage. He also stated that he had never seen any instructions saying that ships in convoy are to zig-zag over 11 knots. He did, however, admit that he had seen a signal saying that ships routed independently are not to zig-zag in new areas. He went on to say that, before convoy KR8 departed from Kilindini, he had been shown a signal ordering that zig-zag manoeuvres should be compulsory north of the Equator and east of 70°, within 200 miles of all coasts except the Persian Gulf.

Ekma's 2nd Officer, Paul Christian Rasmussen, was the next to be called, but his five questions merely concerned what he actually saw of the incident.

* * *

After the retirement of the last witness, the Board inspected various Convoy Instructions and noted in particular 'Instructions for Commodores of Convoys', ICOC 34, Zig-zagging, page 17, paragraph 1. The relevant instructions and advice by the Admiralty as to zig-zagging by convoys can be summarised as follows:

(a) The decision as to whether zig-zagging shall be carried out or not is the responsibility of the Senior Officer of the Escort (C.B.03058, Art. 34).

(b) The Senior Officer of the Escort Forces is responsible for the safety of the convoy from enemy action (C.B.04024, Art. 33a).

(c) Zig-zagging is a useful A/S precaution where the speed of the convoy is sufficient for the zig-zag to be effective. At speeds of less than about 11 knots it is not considered that the resulting security counterbalances the reduction in speed made good (C.B.04024, Art. 170).

* * *

After careful perusal of these documents, the Board called upon Captain Robert Brodie Clark, Master of the *Ellenga*. His observation of the sinking reaffirmed the actual time of the attack. By his watch it was 2.33 pm. When asked about the pre-sailing conference he also confirmed Captain Whiteman's insistence not to zig-zag and added that it had been agreed upon that if Captain Josselyn wanted to zig-zag it would be complied with. An interesting question and answer then came about, as to whether the members of the conference at Kilindini were in favour of zig-zagging. He confirmed that, in his opinion, the general consensus of the conference was not in favour of zig-zagging. He also went on to say that once the personnel had boarded their respective troopship they were not allowed ashore and security was very tight. In his view, there was no possibility of any leakage as to the convoy's destination.

Ellenga's 2nd Officer, Kenneth Powell, was briefly interrogated about what he saw and, when asked if he had observed the enemy submarine's periscope or tracks of the torpedoes, he merely confirmed that he had seen nothing, even though the *Ellenga* had turned towards the direction of the attack.

The Board then interviewed five members of the *Varsova*, which had been abeam on the starboard side of the *Khedive Ismail* and which should have had an unobstructed view of the disaster. However, the first witness, Captain John Walton Knight, had been lying in his cabin when he heard two very loud and distinct explosions. He felt his ship shudder violently. By the time he had run to the bridge the *Khedive Ismail* was practically on her beam ends, enveloped in great clouds of smoke and steam. He saw a portion of her bottom as she went under. He remembered seeing wreckage and the heads of some survivors. There was one lifeboat upright with a solitary person sat in it, whilst three others were upside down and almost completely submerged. Although the helm was hard-a-starboard he swung his ship back into the convoy before turning once more to starboard. He went on to explain that Captain Whiteman was a personal friend of his and that the Chief Officer, John Duncan, and the 3rd Officer, Leonard Lowe (who was lost), were loaned from another ship.

He was then asked about the construction of the *Khedive Ismail*, which he believed to be satisfactory. He also confirmed that he had never known such precautions taken over security before. Twenty-four hours prior to sailing there were two security officers at the gangway and everyone who came aboard or went ashore had to show passes. Captain Knight had been informed in Mombasa, by the Sea Transport Officer and the Naval Control Service Officer, that everything was being done to keep the movement of the convoy secret. He also stated that had security been on any bigger scale it would only have aroused suspicion.

He confirmed that the submarine's periscope had been seen in the wake of the *Varsova* and that the attack was made at a distance of three cables (600 yards). He also confirmed that one of the spent torpedoes looked as though it was a 'surface runner' as there was no wake, 'just a splash – splash – splash'.

The 2nd Officer was the next to be summoned and said that he had just gone to the starboard side of the bridge at approximately 2.35 pm. On looking aft he saw the submarine's periscope for five to ten seconds about 13 feet from the stern of the *Varsova* and crossing over to port. He only saw three torpedoes, one of which struck the *Khedive Ismail* under the bridge, followed by a second which penetrated the boiler room. He never actually saw the torpedoes fired but did see their track just before they struck the Commodore's ship. The third shot across the bows of HMS *Hawkins*.

The three Maritime Royal Artillery gunners were the next to be individually called to the board to give their evidence. They were Eric Clifford Horrell (No. 4626390), Edward William Barber (No. 14224604) and William Jackson (No. 14230499). William Jackson was the first to see the periscope as it emerged on the far quarter of the starboard side, about 50 yards away. All the gunners said that the time was approximately 2.30 pm and that the periscope was protruding by about 2 feet and travelling in a northerly direction, almost at right angles to their own course. They saw it for about five seconds.

The Board adjourned at 12.30 pm on the 16th February and did not resume until the following day at 3.00 pm.

The first person to be interviewed on the afternoon of the 17th February was the Officer of the Watch on board HMS *Hawkins*, Lieutenant John Cuthbert Kemp. When questioned he explained that he was taking a bearing off the *Khedive Ismail* at 14.35 when he witnessed a plume of oil and spray from the troopship's after hold on the starboard side. The second explosion took place very shortly afterwards between her funnel and her mainmast, again on the starboard side. It was of greater intensity than the first and it appeared that one or more of her boilers had blown up. The *Khedive Ismail* then capsized to starboard and sank quickly stern first, the time taken being about three-and-a-quarter minutes. Two further torpedoes passed the Commodore's ship, one under her counter and the other just ahead. The torpedo which passed under her counter surfaced about 50 yards from the starboard bow, leapt out of the water, zig-zagged slightly and resumed a course 50° starboard of its original course. The leading ship of the starboard column was the *Varsova* and she was about 1¼ ship's length off her station, whilst the *Ellenga* was astern of station, in the same column.

The next *Hawkins* person to be cross-examined was the Gunnery Officer, Lieutenant Thomas William Winter. He was also on the bridge of the cruiser at the time of the sinking. Part of his questioning concerned the existence of any signals reporting the position of enemy submarines. His reply confirmed that there were no such signals, nothing had been reported and as far as he knew, there were no submarines in the area.

He was briefly asked his opinion as to whether they should be zig-zagging. His careful reply confirmed that he had been present at all of the discussions concerning the manoeuvre and knew that the policy not to zig-zag had been decided upon. He also knew that further signals would be discussed later.

He was then asked to describe the destroyers' method of screening. He clarified that HMS *Petard* was 30° on the Commodore's starboard bow and HMS *Paladin* was 30° on the port side. The were both weaving about 30° each side of the mean course at a distance of about 2,000 yards.

Lieutenant Robert White, who was the Navigating Officer on board the *Hawkins*, was standing in the chart house when the first explosion occurred. He stated that the enemy submarine, judging by the track of the torpedoes, attacked from Green 120°. He was then asked if the destroyers were asked to zig-zag. He answered no and went on to speak about the conversations with Josselyn, Whiteman and Egan, saying that there had been much concern about spending an extra night at sea and this consideration had swayed the decision to defer zig-zagging.

It was now the turn of Captain John William Josselyn to give his evidence and defend his decisions before that fateful day. He explained that he had been sitting in his sea cabin on the deck below the bridge at the time of the attack.

Because of the importance of the question of zig-zagging, which had become the focal point of the Board of Enquiry, the questions and answers have been included, in full, to give the reader some idea of the nature of the cross-examination.

His opening question was No. 201: 'Will you tell the Board briefly what were your subsequent movements?'

'On hearing the explosions, of which I thought at the time there were three, two loud and one very loud, I went straight out of my door which opened to the starboard side of the lower bridge, and I saw the *Khedive Ismail* on her beam ends at that time. I went onto the bridge and the Officer-of-the-Watch had already given the order "Hard-a-port, full speed ahead" and I noticed the track just passing under our fo'c's'le and I looked to port and it continued there so the torpedo was well to port. Just afterwards I sighted a surface runner which was breaking the surface on our starboard bow as we were swinging to port. Shortly afterwards *Paladin* who was on the port bow of the convoy, *Hawkins* leading the port wing column, carried out an attack slightly on my port bow. I imagine that the Vice-Commodore in *Ekma* seeing this attack thought he had to alter course to starboard and he hoisted and executed the signal for an emergency turn to starboard. By this time I had made sure in my own mind that the submarine was on the starboard side of the convoy, particularly as *Petard* who was on that side reported a periscope about this time, so when the Vice-Commodore altered course to starboard I realised that the two rear ships of the starboard wing and centre column were exposed to danger of another attack so I told the Commodore to resume mean course and proceed at maximum speed which he immediately did. I then found the *Paladin* apparently trying to regain station on the convoy, and in any case I knew that the object which she had attacked could not be the U-boat that had done the damage, so I ordered her to join *Petard* and hunt. While all this was going on *Khedive Ismail* had disappeared sometime previously and I did notice that all traces of the *Khedive Ismail* herself had disappeared some appreciable time before the *Ekma* passed through the survivors.'

Q. 202. 'Were both destroyers zig-zagging?'

'Yes sir.'

Q. 203. 'Had *Paladin* been ordered to do less zig-zag than *Petard* owing to shortage of fuel?'

'Not so far as I know. The Senior Officer of the destroyer in *Petard* had informed me that he would keep the destroyers broadly on the bow.'

Q. 204. 'At the conference you had, before you sailed, it was decided that you would not zig-zag until you had further reconsidered the matter during your voyage?'

'Yes sir.'

Q. 205. 'When had you in mind that you would commence to zig-zag?'

'Originally I had intended to zig-zag on the 11th, but the convoy was about 24 hours adrift, 24 hours astern of station, and the new time would have been 08.00 local time on the 12th.'

Q. 206. 'The new time you would commence to zig-zag?'

'Yes sir.'

Q. 207. 'Why did you not start to zig-zag then?'

'It is explained in my signals and in my report, but the fact was there was no indication of any U-boat nor had there been any indication of a U-boat in that vicinity nor in that area G, and we were 24 hours astern, if we zig-zagged we could not save daylight on the 14th and it would have meant hanging about Colombo for the whole night. I think all the signals are there.' [See Appendices.]

Q. 208. 'Why did you disregard the Instructions for Commodores of Convoys, which says to zig-zag over 11 knots?'

'Those are instructions to Commodores.'

Q. 209. 'Are you familiar with those instructions?'

'I had read them on another occasion. It says in there that it is better to use zig-zags for short times between operations than big alterations of course.'

Q. 210. 'In paragraph 11 of your report it says "I was informed that Commodore and Naval Control Service Officer had decided that the convoy was not to zig-zag"?'

'Yes sir.'

Q. 211. 'In article 34 of ICOC [Instructions for Commodores of Convoys] it lays out the decision as to whether zig-zagging shall be carried out or not is the responsibility of the Senior Officer of the Escort.'

'Yes, I took it it was my responsibility.'

Q. 212. 'You were over-ridden by the Commodore?'

'No. Only I have often taken convoys which did not zig-zag but on this occasion for some reason I was very worried about it, and after arguing at the meeting I agreed with the Commodore that we should not zig-zag to begin with. I would like to say that both the Commander-in-Chief Eastern Fleet's signal and the sailing signal both gave the speed of advance as 13 knots. We could never have made 13 knots speed of advance because the speed of the convoy was that of the slowest ship and the other ships only had a small margin over that. Having decided to agree with the Commodore that we should not zig-zag for the early part of the voyage I went to see the Chief Staff Officer to Flag Officer East Africa and informed him of this, that the Commodore did not intend to zig-zag. Whether he meant what he said in reply, I do not know, but it did influence my mind.'

Q. 213. 'What was his reply to you?'

'He said, so far as I can remember, that there was now a school of thought that said it was not much good zig-zagging with convoys as the two knots or so reduction in speed of advance would help any U-boat to catch up.'

Q. 214. 'Was it clear at the conference that the speed of advance of 13 knots could not possibly be maintained?'

'Quite clear I should think to everybody, not if we zig-zagged.'

Q. 215. 'Is this your letter reporting the circumstances of the sinking of the *Khedive Ismail*?' [Witness was shown letter]

'Yes sir.'

Q. 216. 'Did you have any unusual anxieties in regard to the command of your convoy, air cover, or air escort given you?'

'No sir, but I did not like the One and Half Degree Channel very much, but the anxiety about the One and Half Degree Channel really only arose out of my great anxiety over not zig-zagging.'

Q. 217. 'That worried you all the time?'

'Yes sir.'

Q. 218. 'Did you represent any of your anxieties to a higher authority at Kilindini?'

'No sir. When I left Kilindini, apart from informing the Chief Staff Officer to FOEA [Flag Officer Eastern Area] about not zig-zagging, I had every intention of zig-zagging from about 70° east. It was only the delaying of the convoy and the fact I would have to hang around Colombo for the whole night which altered my decision. Furthermore there is one other small point, the station keeping of the *Varsova* had been extremely bad throughout the convoy and at the conference previously the Captain of the *Varsova* had said he did not want to zig-zag owing to the very great inexperience of his officers of the watch.'

Q. 219. 'Did you consider you were in charge of the convoy apart from its timely arrival and safe conduct?'

'No sir.'

Q. 220. 'Or did you consider the Commodore of the Convoy was the authority in the matter of zig-zagging?'

'Yes, I thought the Commodore was in charge of the convoy but I was well aware that he would depend upon me to advise him or tell him when to zig-zag. I have no illusions that I was the final authority to decide that point.'

Q. 221. 'Are you aware of ICOC [Instructions for Commodores of Convoys] paragraph 34 which reads: "the decision as to whether zig-zagging should be carried out or not is the responsibility of the Senior Officer of the Escort"?'

'I knew it was my responsibility.'

Q. 222. 'Were you satisfied that the destroyers were in their correct stations during the afternoon?'

'Yes.'

Q. 223. 'Is HMS *Hawkins* fitted with ASDICs?'

'No sir.'

Q. 224. 'Did you consider the position occupied by *Hawkins* in the convoy was the best from the point of view of escort to the convoy?'

'Yes, in fact I altered the order of the convoy at the conference in order to put myself there.'

Q. 225. 'Were the screening positions occupied by the destroyers controlled by you or the Senior Officer Destroyers?'

'By the Senior Officer Destroyers.'

Q. 226. 'To the best of your knowledge the destroyers' asdic sets were in full operation during that afternoon?'

'They were never reported out of action.'

Q. 227. 'Had any reports of non-submarine contacts been obtained previous to the torpedoing?'

'None had been reported.'

Q. 228. 'Are you of the opinion that the avoiding action of your officer of the watch avoided one of the torpedoes?'

'I should think his immediate action probably did.'

Q. 229. 'Did you have any grounds to suggest that the sailing and routing of the convoy might have been known to the enemy?'

'No sir.'

Q. 230. 'Briefly, what security measures were taken at Kilindini in regard to the safe sailing of the convoy?'

'I have no knowledge of the measures taken, so far as my ship is concerned the Navigating Officer and I attended the conference, but the "Most Secret" signal from the Commander-in-Chief Eastern Fleet ordering the sailing, and I think the route as well, was seen only by myself and the Commander to start with, and later the Navigating Officer.'

Q. 231. 'How long before you sailed did you have the conference?'

'It was in the afternoon of Friday the 4th and we sailed on the afternoon of the 5th. Of course the conference was ordered by the Eastern Fleet signal and it must be known to all the signalmen if there is a convoy sailing shortly and of course it is also known to all the pilots in the harbour.'

Q. 232. 'Would your destination be known?'

'It was known sir.'

Q. 233. 'How do you mean "it was known"?'

'I had two parcels sent over to me to take off to certain officers here.'

Q. 234. 'A previous witness has said that you made a signal three days before the torpedoing calling the attention to a wireless oscillation, could that have had any bearing on the incident?'

'So far as I can remember that signal came from the Commodore but not being technical I do not know whether it could be heard very far away, I understand only 100 miles or so, but I myself made a signal to

Commander-in-Chief Eastern Fleet on high frequency late on Wednesday the 9th, informing him that we were very late and asking for destroyer escort to meet us early on Friday the 11th at a position farther west than that originally intended.'

Q. 235. 'Did you have destroyer escort all the way?'

'No sir. We had no escort after the two cutters and the small frigate left us on the 9th.'

Q. 236. 'Did you receive the daily submarine report from the Eastern Fleet?'

'Yes, I received all the U-boat disposition reports.'

Q. 237. 'Did the reports indicate any submarine activity in this area?'

'No sir. One previously had said a Japanese U-boat which had been some distance to the south-east of Ceylon might have arrived in area G and the scale of air escort was then increased, but it was reduced before the disaster, and in the meantime another Japanese U-boat had been reported on the east coast of India, and in my own mind I thought it possible that the one to the south-east of Ceylon had gone there.'

There was no further questioning and Captain Josselyn withdrew.

The next officer to be called was Lieutenant Roger Cecil Morgan. He was the Navigating Officer of HMS *Paladin*. He was in the destroyer's wardroom at the time of the attack. By the time he had rushed up on deck he could only see the bows of the *Khedive Ismail* and as soon as he had got to the bridge the troopship had already submerged.

His interrogation included questions about the condition of the asdic apparatus which he confirmed, to the best of his knowledge, was working correctly. He was also questioned about the depth-charging which he admitted had taken place whilst survivors were in the water. He stated that, in his opinion, all the survivors were either in boats or on rafts and was pretty sure that the attacks by HMS *Paladin* had no effect on them at all.

The *Khedive Ismail*'s Chief Officer, John Duncan, who had joined the troopship only 3½ months before the sinking, was the next to be called. He, like many of the other witnesses, was asked to give his version of the sequence of events. He was also asked about the general condition of the ship. He said that for a ship that was 22 years old she was in pretty good trim and there was very little rust. In fact, the ship had undergone an extensive three-month survey at Port Elizabeth, South Africa, in March 1943.

He was also asked if he thought there were any precautions that could have been taken to retard the ship's demise. He explained that the chain of events was too swift to do anything and as far as he was aware the two warheads struck in and around the engine room. He also stated that all the lifeboats that were on the boat deck as well as 36 rafts broke free or were blown off the afflicted ship.

Another survivor from the *Khedive Ismail*, her 2nd Officer, Cecil Munday, was then called. He had probably been the last person to see Captain Whiteman alive: he was clinging to the inside of the rail shouting instructions to the remainder of the people he could see. Cecil Munday had joined the *Khedive Ismail* in June 1943. He went on to explain that he had seen the periscope seconds before the first explosion. It was protruding about four feet above the surface and was near the wake of the *Varsova*, moving towards the *Khedive Ismail*. He also remarked on the heroic conduct of all the survivors.

Having finished with the interrogation of all the eye-witnesses the Board then summoned the Chief-of-Staff, Eastern Fleet who was based at HMS *Lanka*, Ceylon. He was Ralph Alan Bevan Edwards, CBE, a Commodore, First Class. He was asked whether he considered that two destroyers were sufficient to protect five troopships under prevailing conditions. He replied that initially there were supposed to be three A/S escorts but HMS *Penn* had unfortunately broken down and was therefore unavailable for duty. The only other ship available at that time had just finished boiler cleaning and was at Trincomalee. Air escort had not been provided and neither would it, unless there was good reason to expect the presence of a U-boat in that area. In this case there had been no indication that an enemy U-boat was present.

The last person to be called upon was Captain Gerald Seymour Tuck, DSO, who was also stationed at HMS *Lanka* and was Captain (O) on the staff of Commander-in-Chief, Eastern Fleet. He, like the previous interviewee, was asked about the strength of the escort ships available at Ceylon. He stated that, more often than not, troop convoys could only be given two, or sometimes three, frigates or corvettes.

The only air escort that could have been provided were two Catalinas which could have been flown to Addu Atoll on the 11th. However, it was considered that the movement of a floating dock, which was en route to Trincomalee on the 12th, and the presence of units at sea, east of Ceylon, were a greater priority.

The Board of Enquiry was typed up and despatched to Admiral Somerville.

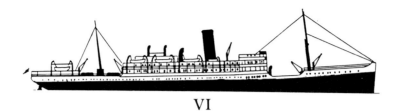

VI

THE FINDINGS OF THE BOARD OF ENQUIRY

The conclusions of the Board of Enquiry were sent to the Commander-in-Chief, Admiral Sir James Somerville in a 'Secret' letter, No. C.03214 dated 19th February 1944. It read as follows:

Sir,

In accordance with the instructions contained in your Memorandum dated 15th February 1944, we have held a full and careful enquiry into the circumstances attending the loss of the troopship *Khedive Ismail* on Saturday 12th February 1944 and we find with particular reference to the points specified in paragraph 2 therein, that:

(a) The A/S escort consisted of two asdic fitted destroyers, HM Ships *Petard* and *Paladin* and the ocean escort was provided by one cruiser, HMS *Hawkins,* which was non-asdic fitted. The provision of only two A/S escorts for such a valuable convoy, five troopships carrying a total of 6,311 men were present, is not considered to have been sufficient to ensure adequate protection against U-boat attack. In fact, however, a third A/S escort, the asdic fitted destroyer, HMS *Penn* had also been detailed for this duty but was prevented from joining owing to defects. The Board is of the opinion that the A/S escort could not have been increased from the escort resources available on station.

(b) Air escort could have been provided but at the expense of air strikes or hunts to exhaustion, for which purposes the available aircraft were being reserved.

(c) The convoy disposition of three columns of two ships, each three cables apart, is considered to have been correct. The A/S escorts were disposed 3,000 yards, 45° on either bow of the convoy, speed 16 knots, and carrying out a broad zig-zag to cover the front. Although a small gap was left ahead of the convoy this disposition is considered to have been a good compromise against both close and long range attacks. The convoy was on a steady course of 073°, speed 13 knots, not zig-zagging.

(d) There is no evidence available to suggest that the rapid sinking of the *Khedive Ismail* can in any way be attributed to her particular construction or that she was in any other than a well found condition. She was hit by two well-placed shots in a vital part of the ship, apparently in the vicinity of the engine and boiler rooms. There is indication there was a boiler explosion and the rapid sinking must be attributed to this cause.

(e) There are no grounds to suggest that any breach of security resulted in the sailing and routeing of the convoy being known.

2. In amplification the Board considers:

(i) That the troopship *Khedive Ismail* was sunk by two torpedoes being part of a salvo of four fired by an enemy submarine in approximate position, latitude 00° 52′ N, longitude 72° 14′ E at 14.35 (local time) 09.05 GMT on 12th February 1944.

(ii) That the enemy submarine fired from a position slightly abaft the starboard beam of the *Khedive Ismail* at a range approximately 800 yards, which position was close to the starboard quarter of the troopship *Varsova*.

(iii) The narratives and reports forwarded by the Commanding Officers of HM Ships *Hawkins, Petard* and *Paladin* attached to this report are correct in all essential points and are confirmed by the evidence. [See Appendices for Commanding Officers' reports.]

(iv) Sketch 'B' is considered to represent closely the order of the convoy at the time of the attack. [See picture No. 20.]

(v) No asdic contact was obtained prior to the incident, and from the reported positions of periscope sightings at the time at which the U-boat fired the torpedoes, it appears probable that the U-boat sighted the convoy within the limiting lines of approach, approached directly from ahead on an opposite course to the convoy, below periscope depth and passed undetected inside the starboard A/S escort close to the convoy track. She turned towards and raised her periscope for a 'snap shot' at very close range.

3. With regard to the protection of this convoy, the Board are of the opinion that the decision to withhold the very limited available aircraft at this stage was correct in view of other known commitments close to Ceylon and in the Bay of Bengal. These commitments were the very vulnerable floating dock on passage to Trincomalee and the movements of units of the Fleet in the Bay of Bengal. The absence of any indication of submarine activity west of the Maldives justified the decision not to send these aircraft to this area 700 miles to the south-west of Ceylon.

In this matter the Board wish to record their opinion that the present numbers of escort vessels and escort aircraft on the Station is totally inadequate for the efficient protection of the valuable convoys on widely separated routes.

PASSAGE TO DESTINY

In the case of this particular convoy there was a period of 48 hours when there was no A/S escort whatever, and at no time were there more than two asdic-fitted vessels.

4. The matter of the steering of a steady course by the Convoy was carefully studied. The Senior Officer of Escort [Captain Josselyn of HMS *Hawkins*] came to his decision not to zig-zag deliberately and after much thought and after discussion both at the conference and by signal with the Commodore of the Convoy. It is beyond question that any zig-zag would have resulted in a delay of the convoy, amounting to an additional night at sea in potentially dangerous waters, and Captain Josselyn fully appreciated this, as he did the fact that no submarine warnings were in force.

In the opinion of the Board his decision, made in no haste and with no negligence, was the incorrect one, placing as it did an undue reliance on the A/S powers of an inadequate escort and over-stressing the additional danger of an extra night at sea.

In the opinion of the Board the risks attending a convoy in formation steering a steady course at 13 knots in clear weather with a calm sea outweigh other risks and justify a reduction of speed of advance. The fact that a submarine was able to make an undetected close-range attack from the beam clearly indicates the dangers of this procedure and it must be pointed out that for two days the Convoy had been without any A/S escort and had during that period to rely solely on look-outs from HMS *Hawkins* which was then zig-zagging ahead.

5. The evidence of the Chief Officer, John Duncan, was conclusive that the structural qualities of the troopship *Khedive Ismail* were in all aspects up to standard.

It is quite clear that the speed at which the ship sank rendered any attempt at organised abandoning an absolute impossibility, and it is also evident that those who happened to be between decks had little or no chance whatsoever of leaving the ship.

The conduct of all in the water was evidently of a high standard.

6. We find also that the Vice-Commodore, Captain Denys Gun-Cuninghame, of the troopship *Ekma* took charge promptly and efficiently, and that the manoeuvres of the ships of the convoy after the attack conformed to regular procedure according to signals displayed.

We have the honour to be, Sir, Your obedient Servants, Signed:

C. W. North, Lieutenant-Commander, Royal Navy. Fleet A/S Officer; C. A. Merriman, Captain, Royal Navy. Chief Staff Officer to Flag Officer, Ceylon; R. S. G. Nicholson, PRESIDENT [of the Board] Rear-Admiral, Flag Officer, Ceylon.

* * *

FINDINGS OF THE BOARD OF ENQUIRY

Admiral Somerville appended his reply to the Findings in a document headed 'Eastern Fleet, Most Secret, Ref. No. 422/EF/716/H/55, dated 29th February 1944', which runs as follows:

(Copy to: Flag Officer, Ceylon). Forwarded for Their Lordships' information.

2. My comments on the finding of the Board of Enquiry are as follows:

Paragraph 1 (a).

I concur that the A/S escort of the convoy was inadequate. This inadequacy was due to the following considerations:

(i) At the time in question there was no indication of the presence or probable presence of enemy submarines in this area. With the information available it appeared that any Japanese submarines proceeding from Penang to the westward would probably keep south of Ceylon and north of the equator to attack shipping in the Arabian Sea. Apart from this, Japanese submarines had shown a marked disinclination to attack escorted convoys.

(ii) Admiralty Message 02 2256/January, indicated an intention that *Renown, Illustrious* and other units of the Fleet would proceed to the Pacific towards the end of March. In consequence, it was decided to retain, if possible, 7 destroyers at Trincomalee in order that the Fleet might carry out exercises which the Vice-Admiral, Second-in-Command considered essential if this detachment to the Pacific was to achieve a proper standard of fighting efficiency before their arrival in Australian waters.

(iii) The remaining 17 destroyers allotted to the Eastern Fleet were engaged as follows on the 7th February, the date on which Convoy KR8 sailed from Kilindini [KR8 actually sailed on 5th February] and on the 12th February the date on which the *Khedive Ismail* was sunk:

	In Harbour	At Sea
With the Fleet	5	7
Operation 'Canned'	1	1
Convoy escort (inc. KR8)	3	5
Off station on passage to Eastern Fleet	5	5
At Fleet base, boiler cleaning and/or defects	3	0
At other ports, docking and/or refits	5	1
Refitting at, or proceeding to South Africa	2	2
In harbour	0	3 (Trincomalee)
Totals	24	24

(iv) It had been intended to sail HMS *Penn* from Colombo to supplement the escort of KR8 before the latter's arrival at the One and Half Degree Channel, but this ship developed defects and was unable to proceed.

3. On the 9th February, a signal was received from the Commander-in-Chief, Army Group, South East Asia Command, requesting that Naval action should be taken to contain a Japanese division in the Ramree area in order to ease the situation in the Arakan. I proceeded by air to Trincomalee on the 10th February to discuss the situation with the Vice-Admiral, Second-in-Command, and decided that a demonstration by units of the Fleet in the Bay of Bengal provided the only practical means of giving support to the Army. For this movement I considered 7 destroyers were necessary in view of the presence of Japanese submarines off the east coast of India. Since the reactions of the Japanese and the possible need of the movement being extended could not be forecasted, I approved the movement of *Penn* and two other destroyers to Trincomalee to meet eventualities.

4. In the light of the foregoing I consider that any increase of the destroyer escort for KR8 could only have been obtained at the expense of other commitments that appeared to have priority.

5. Paragraph 1 (b).
Although at the time a submarine threat was known to exist on the east coast of India and although it was particularly desired to conserve air forces to enable an effective search and strike to be made against enemy submarines in this area, I now consider that too much weight was attached to the prospective operation and that the air escort arranged for the night and day passage of KR8 after passing through the One and Half Degree Channel should have been extended to cover the approach to the channel. I accept full responsibility and consider I was at fault in not arranging for this possible additional insurance for the safety of the convoy.
6. Paragraphs 1 (c), (d), (e). I concur.

7. Paragraph 3. In spite of the additional commitments referred to, I adhere to the opinions expressed in my paragraph 4.

8. Paragraph 4. I concur and consider that Captain J. W. Josselyn, RN, committed an error of judgement in deciding not to zig-zag, although I fully appreciate that the right decision was by no means obvious and may still be a matter of opinion in view of the known possibility of submarine attack east of the Maldives and the apparent freedom from attack to the westward of these islands. I have not informed Captain Josselyn of my opinion pending receipt of their Lordships' views.

9. Paragraphs 5 and 6. I concur.

Signed

J. F. Somerville ADMIRAL.

FINDINGS OF THE BOARD OF ENQUIRY

In a general comment from A. Nicholl, Director of Defence (F), dated 13th April 1944 the following comment was made:

> There is a shortage of fast A/S escorts in the Eastern Theatre and risks have had to be taken. Troop convoys will tend to increase during the next few months and while the fast A/S escort situation is expected to improve very slightly, no great improvement can be expected until after Operation Overlord has been completed.

* * *

With reference to HMS *Petard*'s torpedo action against the Japanese submarine *I-27* G. S. Sayers (for the Director of Tactical, Torpedo and Staff Duties Division or DTSD) recorded the following statement on 12th May 1944:

> It is considered that *Petard* was wrong to fire torpedoes singly at the surfaced U-boat (para. 19 of *Petard*'s No. 01/2856 dated 16th February 1944). DTSD concurs in the remarks of Commodore (D) Eastern Fleet on this point, viz. that a salvo of four torpedoes fired with a narrow spread would have been more effective.

* * *

In a 'TOP SECRET' typed letter addressed to the Commander-in-Chief, Admiral Somerville, dated 2nd September 1944, the following was recorded Re: N.L./M.056375/44:

> I am to refer to your submission No. 422/E.F.716/H/55 dated 29th February 1944, concerning the Findings of the Board of Enquiry into the circumstances attending the loss of the troopship *Khedive Ismail.*
>
> 2. I am to inform you that Their Lordships consider that the Commanding Officer, HMS *Hawkins* committed an initial error of judgement in that he accepted the 13 knot advance schedule for his convoy which left no time in hand for zig-zagging.
>
> 3. In the event, the convoy made somewhat less than its planned advance which would have involved an additional night at sea if the avowed intention, to zig-zag from about 70 degrees east, had been put into operation. In that the daily U-boat appreciations for the period 8th to 12th February pointed to the possible presence of a U-boat in a potentially dangerous area, Their Lordships consider that the decision of the Commanding Officer (HMS *Hawkins*) to dispense with the elementary A/S precaution of zig-zagging to avoid extra time at sea was a further error of judgment.
>
> 4. In connection with the responsibility of the Senior Officer of the Escort to order zig-zagging as necessary (CB 03058 Art. 34 refers), I am to invite attention to the incorrect and misleading replies given by the Naval Control

Service Officer, Colombo to questions 45, 46 and 47 by the Board of Enquiry.

5. Their Lordships' views are being communicated to Captain Josselyn direct.

BY COMMAND OF THEIR LORDSHIPS

Signed

H. V. MARKHAM

(Despatched on the 4th September 1944).

(Questions 45, 46 and 47, quoted in the previous letter Re: No. 4 were directed at Commander Arthur Guy Denis Bagot. They are included forthwith:

Q. 45. What are the Standing Orders which govern zig-zagging of a convoy?

Ships with a speed of 11 knots and over are to zig-zag when in company as laid down on Convoy Instructions.

Q. 46. Who decides the zig-zagging policy?

It is discussed at the conference and between the Commodore and the Naval Control Service Officer with the Senior Officer of the Escort present.

Q. 47. Who gives the ruling after that discussion?

The Naval Control Service Officer.)

* * *

On the same day a 'TOP SECRET & PERSONAL' letter was despatched to Captain Josselyn, which read:

Sir,

I am commanded by the Lords Commissioners of the Admiralty to refer to the Board of Enquiry held to investigate the loss of SS *Khedive Ismail* on 12th February 1944, and to inform you that in their opinion you committed an initial error of judgment in that you accepted the 13 knot advance schedule for the convoy which left no time in hand for zig-zagging.

In the event, the convoy made somewhat less than its planned advance which would have involved an additional night at sea if the avowed intention to zig-zag from about 70° east had been put into operation. In that the daily U-boat appreciations for the period 8th – 12th February pointed to the possible presence of a U-boat in a potentially dangerous area, My Lords consider that your decision to dispense with the elementary A/S precaution of zig-zagging to avoid extra time at sea was a further error of judgment.

I am, Sir, Your obedient Servant, H. V. Markham.

FINDINGS OF THE BOARD OF ENQUIRY

When all the letters and evidence in both this and the preceding chapter are studied, one thing does become clear, even allowing for the way in which the Eastern Fleet's resources were over-stretched: the safety of fleet manoeuvres and the movement of important equipment took precedence over the safety of human lives. Despite the large number of troops and the rare passage of many female personnel, the Admiralty only found it possible to provide two A/S destroyers for KR8. Indeed, for just over twenty-four hours the convoy's security depended on the vigilance of only one cruiser, which was not fitted with asdic equipment. No doubt there would have been greater recriminations if more ships had been sunk, but it is doubtful whether any further protection or greater precaution would have saved more lives: the attack took place when the convoy was enjoying its greatest degree of protection. Aspects of the zig-zag manoeuvre could have provided the enemy with opportunities to attack: if the starboard wing A/S destroyer, HMS *Petard*, had been on the port leg of its 30° zig-zag the enemy submarine could have glided in from ahead without detection. Once through the screen, the rest of the attack was relatively simple, providing it was carried out quickly.

The Admiralty had carefully worded its instructions. At no time during the War did they order that all ships in convoy, travelling at 11 knots or over, must zig-zag at all times, because they knew that there were pros and cons to the tactic. Nevertheless, if something went wrong, the Admiralty still took the trouble to issue reprimands such as that given to Captain Josselyn.

The signals which were being broadcast daily by the staff of the Commander-in-Chief, Eastern Fleet are another area appropriate for criticism. By issuing the unreliable information that there were no enemy U-boats reported in Area G, the area that convoy KR8 had just entered, the broadcasters created a situation which was worse than if they had said nothing at all, because it invited the captains at sea to relax their vigilance. (See Appendices for the signals concerning U-boat appreciations.)

* * *

Any theory as to why the troopship sank so rapidly will be almost entirely conjectural. However, by studying both the ship's plans and using the eye-witness accounts, a reasonable picture can be painted. Let us use Clifford Horrell's account first, as he was in the ideal position to witness the chain of events as they happened. After sighting the dark green periscope he saw the first torpedo strike between the third and fourth lifeboats, shortly followed by the second, which struck directly below the ship's funnel. The first incursion was a direct hit, right in the centre of the engine

40. Cliff Horrell, SS *Varsova*, gunner and one of the key eye-witnesses to the sinking of the troopship *Khedive Ismail*.

room and almost certainly broached the after bulkhead and the intervening deckhead adjoining No. 3 hold. This is a very reasonable assumption as one army survivor saw the after hatch covers blown off and the main stairway collapse.

The second torpedo struck several feet higher, due to the increasing list caused by the first detonation, and tore into the heart of the ship's six boilers which, at full working pressure, would have compounded the explosion, greatly weakening the ship's bottom and almost certainly holing the forward bulkhead of No. 2 hold. It also blew a large hole in the boatdeck. The combination of the two well-placed warheads greatly weakened the starboard side of the transport and almost certainly blew out the six coal bunker loading hatch doors (three each side) which had never been removed, even though she had been converted to fuel oil shortly before completion.

As the stricken ship started to sink by the stern and rolled onto her beam ends, still moving forward, water gushed into the forward and after holds, skylight, and accommodation entrances, and probably even through the shaft tunnels and many other apertures and compartments. The massive inrush of water tore the after portion of the ship from the forward section breaking it in two. The effect was dramatic as the open part of the severed after end scooped up tons of water, deepening every second until the stern lifted at an angle and slid beneath the waves. Meanwhile, the forward end, being somewhat streamlined by the shape of her undamaged bow, glided along, deepening aft until it stopped in a vertical position, poised for a fraction of a second, before sinking in a spiral motion.

Anyone trying to gain exit through the passageways of the main deck would be almost immediately limited to the rear exits, if they were in the rear half of the ship, or the forward exits if they were at the front, because the damage at the centre would have presented an insuperable obstacle of chaos. Once the ship was on her beam ends, they would also be trapped by the decks forming vertical, unclimbable walls. Most of the survivors who did escape were either blown off the ship by the initial explosions or were already on deck and able to jump into the sea, or they managed to scramble through open portholes and run down the exposed side. Attempts to abandon ship were further hampered by falling lifeboats, masts and superstructure. Appropriate decisions had to be made immediately and once acted upon, were final. One hundred seconds does not favour the passengers' chances of survival.

* * *

Gloria Smith (*née* West) still remembers feeling very depressed immediately after the incident, but she will never forget the moment of absolute amazement when she realised that she had survived. In 1946 she was demobbed in South Africa, after serving in Ceylon, and married in Kenya during April of the same year. In 1948 their only child, Maureen, was born in Nairobi. Whilst her husband plied his skills on various civil engineering projects, they lived in Kenya, Tanganyika and Uganda. However, due to political unrest in Uganda they moved to Somerset West, South Africa, in 1967. Sadly she lost her husband in 1987 and now lives near her daughter in Durbanville, near Cape Town. It was not until her daughter asked her about the event, some forty years after, that Gloria decided to record her memories. Her day-to-day experiences were compiled from some skimpy authentic notes that she had taken at the time and kept ever since.

* * *

Phyllis Hutchinson ('Hutch' to her friends) wrote several accounts of her experience on that fateful day and stayed in Africa for 15 years, ending up as a hospital matron. She was born in Lincolnshire and had started her

41–42. Gloria Smith (*née* West). Photographed on 25th July 1943, and more recently on the Great Wall of China.

nursing career in 1930 at the Lincoln County Hospital, and was eventually awarded the MBE for her services in Nyasaland, finishing her last 17 working years as a Health Visitor in the Mablethorpe district of Lincolnshire. She was a remarkable woman and, before the *Khedive Ismail* incident, had climbed to the peak of Kilimanjaro, becoming the second woman to do so. She died several years ago.

* * *

After recovery from his broken leg, Buster was drafted to HMS *Resource*, a fleet repair ship. He was finally demobbed in late 1946 after completing his twelve years service. Shortly after, he started working for a fertiliser manufacturer, in Avonmouth, called Fisons. Ironically, he became a boilerman and eventually retired in 1981. He had married Vera Joyce Hunt on 7th October 1939 and they had two sons, Rodney and Brian. He was always a cheerful person, whom everybody liked, and he considered every day after the 12th February 1944 a bonus.

43. Buster, with his wife Vera, in the summer of 1982.

Bill Howard was married and they had three children, two boys and a girl. He eventually became a very successful industrial engineer for a major gas-producing company before his eventual retirement. The author was able to interview him before his recent death, and came to feel that he had known him all his life, so enriched was he by their only meeting. He was a modest and wonderful gentleman.

* * *

Norah Munro (who was known as 'Rio' to her friends, because she was born in Brazil and the name seemed to reflect her lively and cheerful personality) was 22 years old at the time of the sinking. She married an Army officer, who was in the Argyll and Sutherland Regiment, on Christmas Day 1943, at Mombasa Cathedral. She had joined the WRNS to be near him but he was sent out to Burma. However, their paths did cross some weeks after her safe arrival in Colombo, when he was being shipped back to East Africa to train more African soldiers in the use of small arms. At the end of the War, Norah went back to Brazil along with her husband. She gave birth to a baby boy in 1945 whom they named Howard after Bill Howard, who had so bravely saved her. Unfortunately, due to terrible headaches which

105

44. Bill Howard at Bob and Maureen Macaire's home in Taplow, after being interviewed on Saturday, 3rd September 1994.

were always attributed to her being struck on the head by surface-bound flotsam from the *Khedive Ismail*, she was compelled to return to England to seek better medical attention. Tragically, she died in 1949, just five years after her miraculous survival.

* * *

Dan Docwra stayed in the Royal Marines until 1953. He had been compelled to do an extra two years because of the war in Korea. He married Eileen just after the Second World War and they had six children, four girls and two boys. Whilst he had served in the Royal Marines he had learnt the skills of butchery and worked at a local butcher's shop in Plymouth for many years. When he reached his mid-fifties he worked at Devonport dockyard from where he eventually retired. His wife died just over a year before he did.

* * *

After two weeks survival leave Eddie Turner worked at the Admiralty War Office at HMS *Lanka*. He carried out signal duties whilst living in Colombo. He stayed on in the Royal Navy until 1948, married Doreen on 26th March 1949 and had three daughters. He eventually passed his City & Guilds

45. Dan Docwra when the author met him in August, 1994.

examinations and worked as a builder and decorator, forming a successful business partnership with a friend. He and his wife are now enjoying retirement and live in North Devon.

* * *

Tom Fox finished his 'hostilities only' service in September 1946. He had married Dorothy on the 22nd February the same year. He then went on to learn the skills of accountancy before celebrating the birth of their only son, Roger, in 1952. He eventually ran a successful glazing company with a partner from 1964 until 1986. He now enjoys retirement with his wife.

Unfortunately, Tom Fox's mother was sent an official RN telegram followed by a letter a few days later, stating that he had been lost through enemy action. When he tried to get demobbed at the end of the war he was informed that his papers had been mislaid, and he was not demobbed until the end of 1946. He is convinced that his papers had been mistakenly placed in the 'discharged dead file'. The same sort of mistake happened in the case of his good friend Geoff Binns. The latter's parents were first told by an official RN telegram that their son had survived the ordeal. Days later they received a letter telling them that he had been killed at sea.

* * *

46. Eddie Turner at his home in Torrington, North Devon, in May 1996.

R.N.Barracks,
Chatham,
22nd February, 1944.

Dear Madam,

        In confirmation of the telegram already
sent to you, I deeply regret to have to inform
you that your son, Thomas Benjamin Fox,
(Ordinary Coder, C/JX.609705), has been
reported as missing,presumed killed, while
on war service, on 12th February 1944.
        The casualty occurred when the ship
in which he was taking passage was lost
through enemy action.
        There can, I fear, be no hope that
your son is still alive and I should, therefore,
like to express, on behalf of the officers
and men of the Royal Navy, the high traditions
of which your son helped to maintain,
sincere sympathy with you in your sad
bereavement.
        I am, Madam,

        Yours sincerely,

47. Typed letter sent to Mrs Fox.

Patrick Breen had joined the Army, before the outbreak of the war, as a
bombardier (gunner) in the Royal Artillery Regiment. As soon as hostilities
started he was sent over to France with the British Expeditionary Forces.
After escaping capture at Dunkirk he was then sent to North Africa and on

into Ethiopia (Abyssinia), before being sent to 301st Field Regiment in Kenya, along with many more from his Regiment. Here, he was promoted to Sergeant and deployed to train black African troops in preparation for an eventual push into Japanese-occupied Burma. He was transported on the SS *Khedive Ismail* and lost on that fateful day in mid-February, 1944. Mrs Breen was only told of her husband's loss several weeks later. It was usual to send a telegram which was then delivered by a local policeman, but in her case, she simply received the following brief notice:

No. 323745 (Effects)

Effects Form 100 B—2

NOTIFICATION OF DEATH.

CERTIFIED that having regard to such information as is available concerning *No 83682 Sergeant*

Patrick Breen   Royal Artillery

who was officially reported missing, it has been presumed by the War Office that he ~~died~~ was killed in action on *12th February 1944*

~~in~~ *at sea*   ~~while serving with the~~

~~————————————————————————————— Force.~~

Dated this   *5*   day of   *April*   1944

Signed   *V Russell*

The War Office.

(263/613) Wt. 52984/6090   8m 3/43 L. B. & Co. Ltd.   38/5

48. Form 100 B-2, sent to Mrs Breen.

49. Three members of the Royal Artillery prior to sailing on the *Khedive Ismail*.
Patrick Breen is on the right of the picture.

Roy Henbest, who had previously attended the Sea Cadet Corps, voluntarily joined the Royal Navy in early 1943 as an Ordinary Telegraphist. His subsequent training period saw his eventual draft to the shore establishment HMS *Lanka* in Ceylon – hence his inclusion in the complement of the ill-fated liner. He died at the age of 18 years and 2 months. His certificate from the Inspector of Seamen's Wills records a typical payment to the next-of-kin at the time.

50. Certificate sent to Mrs Eva Henbest.   51. Ordinary Telegraphist Roy Henbest, RN.

Survivors and the relatives of the deceased alike would always remember the fateful day on the 12th February, 1944, when so many young people lost their lives.

52–3. Maureen Macaire, Tom Fox and the author on 13th February 1994, after the Wrens' Memorial Service in London; and, below, the memorial to all the Women's Transport/Territorial Service who were killed in the war. It is set on the north wall of St Paul's Church, Wilton Place, Knightsbridge and was unveiled in 1948.

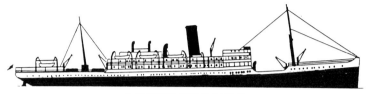

APPENDICES

APPENDIX 1

COMPARISON OF WARSHIPS INVOLVED IN AFTERMATH OF CONVOY KR8 WITH GERMAN TYPE 7c U-boat

Details	Petard/Paladin	Japanese U-boat I-27	German 7c U-boat
Length	345 feet	356 feet	220 feet
Beam	35 feet	30 feet	20 feet
Draft	9 feet	17 feet	16 feet
Std. Disp.	1,800 tons	2,198 tons	761 tons
Speed	36½ knots	23½ knots	17 knots
Submerged	—	8 knots	7½ knots
Complement	210 men	94 men	44 men
Depth	—	330 feet	490/590 feet
Tubes	8	6 bow	4 bow 2 stern
Torpedoes	8	17	14
Main Armament	3x4-inch	1x5.5-inch	1x88mm
Secondary	4x2-pdr.AA 3x40mm AA	2x25mm AA	1x20mm canon
Propulsion	2 steam turbine	2 diesels	2 diesels
Total SHP	40,000	12,400	2,800
Range	—	14,000 n.miles @ 16 knots (surfaced)	6,500 n.miles @ 12 knots (surfaced)
Range (submerged)	—	96 n.miles @ 3 knots	80 n.miles @ 4 knots

APPENDIX 2

ALLIED SHIPPING SUNK BY JAPANESE SUBMARINE I-27

DATE/TIME		SHIP	TONNAGE	POSITION
Captain Yoshimura				
4/6/42		*Barwon*	4,239	45 miles SE of Gabo Island
4/6/42		*Iron Crown*	3,353	38° 17´S 149° 44´E

Total Tonnage Sunk – 7,592 tons

Captain Kitamura				
22/10/42		*Ocean Vintage*	7,174	21° 37´N 60° 06´E

Total Tonnage Sunk – 7,174 tons

Captain Fukumura				
20/3/43		*Fort Mumford*	7,132	10° 00´N 71° 00´E
7/5/43	(05.56)	*Berakit*	6,608	03° 40´N 72° 20´E
3/6/43	(07.35)	*Montanan*	4,898	17° 54´N 58° 09´E
24/6/43	(05.00)	*British Venture*	4,696	25° 13´N 58° 02´E
28/6/43	(04.05)	*Dah Pu*	1,974	Muscat Harbour
5/7/43	(06.10)	*Alcoa Prospector*	6,797	24° 21´N 59° 04´E
7/9/43		*Lyman Stewart*	7,176	03° 30´N 75° 00´E
9/9/43		*Larchbank*	5,151	07° 38´N 74° 00´E
10/10/43		*Sambo*	7,176	12° 28´N 43° 31´E
18/10/43		*Sambridge*	7,176	11° 25´N 47° 25´E
29/10/43	(16.30)	*Athina Livanos*	4,824	12° 20´N 44° 00´E
2/12/43		*Nitsa*	4,732	11° 42´N 45° 32´E
3/12/43		*Fort Camosun*	7,126	11° 23´N 46° 03´E
12/2/44	(14.35)	*Khedive Ismail*	7,513	00° 57´N 72° 16´E

Total Tonnage Sunk – 82,979 tons

Tonnage sunk by all three captains – 97,745 tons

APPENDIX 3

KNOWN EAST AFRICAN PERSONNEL MISSING

301st Field Regiment, East African Artillery

NAME	RANK/NUMBER	NAME	RANK/NUMBER
Abare Songa	Gnr/G/3062	Abdaliah Selemani	Gnr/DT/7606
Abdula Muhamudu	Gnr/N/30076	Abdul Mohamed	Gnr/DT/6728
Abkar Alam Bastay	Gnr/L/50427	Abol Opondo	Gnr/N/6893
Abudoni Owero	L/Bdr/N/6326	Adiriyani Ngobi	Gnr/L/50722
Adrianosekaki	Gnr/DT/7630	Adulai Anyuli	Gnr/N/6407
Adulufukanyike	Gnr/22463	Agonya Menya	Gnr/L/5808
Ahmed Abakar	Bdr/L/50442	Ahmed Mohamed	Gnr/L/50428
Ahmed Harun	Gnr/L/50441	Ahmed Othman	Gnr/L/50435
Ahmed Mohamed	Gnr/L/50438	Akal Morongo	Gnr/46629
Akombe Ogema	L/Bdr/7534	Akuku Nyalual	Crfmn/29860
Albert Mpangala	Gnr/DT/7718	Alfani Ndagile	Bsm/3736
Alfred Kaondo	Gnr/DT/7138	Ali Abdalla	Gnr/L/50389
Ali Athumani	Gnr/DT/8563	Ali Hamisi	Bdr/7813
Ali Mjomu	Gnr/53982	Ali Mohamed	Gnr/N/22372
Alois Masinde	Gnr/DT/7126	Ambeba Ofuoko	Gnr/G/3435
Ambenji Kwemenza	Gnr/L/20188	Ambeyi Lukano	Gnr/23010
Amisi Ammos	L/Bdr/51155	Ammon Kakaga	Gnr/DT/6291
Nkonamango	L/Bdr/7726	Amoka Ocen	Gnr/N/11745
Amonia Rothar	L/Bd/10709	Anayngo Onura	Gnr/21839
Anderea Aneselem	Gnr /49908	Anderea Lukwago	Gnr/57457
Chandaruma	Gnr/DT/10704	Angotoko Auanya	Gnr/N/9736
Antonio Jalafoyo	Gnr/N/11523	Antonio Lwanga	L/Bdr/51182
Anton Kasper	Gnr/DT/7136	Anyegile Buja	L/Bdr/7725
Archie Ngoyo	Gnr/DT/7398	Arnesti Kuta	Bdr/N/6923
Asafu Namunungu	Gnr/L/51181	Asilia Chacha	Gnr/43051
Asmani Sasya	Gnr/L/50245	Asoni Aguch	Gnr/N/9831
Asumani Fadimulla	Pte/N/1916	Asumani Karisha	Gnr/DT/7504
Asumani Kinbulu	Gnr/DT/10692	Asumani Pazi	Gnr/L/180751
Atanasio Okello	Gnr/N/6277	Atosi Gwox	L/Bd/L/51120
Awusa Likadi	Pte/45210	Azin Matayo	Gnr/L/51111

114

APPENDICES

Bahala Kayegesi	Gnr/DT/10645	Balikira Ibrahim	Gnr/L/50433
Barasa Okwaro	Gnr/DT/7538	Baraza Mgondi	Gnr/190075
Barnaba Issa	Bdr/DT/7430	Barnaba Jowi	L/Bdr/7537
Benedict Msafiri	Gnr/DT/10705	Benjamin Angiemda	L/Bdr/Ut/104
Benyamin Opoke	Gnr/L/51091	Bido Chilu	Gnr/DT/10577
Bitentio Odong	Gnr/51769	Boniface Cassian	Gnr/DT/7403
Bundala Kikonoka	Gnr/DT/10744	Bundala Ngasa	Gnr/DT/10744
Bushiri Mohamed	Gnr/DT/10760	Chacha Marwa	Gnr/DT/7646
Chacha Mwita	Gnr/DT/10223	Chacha Saye	Gnr/DT/10652
Chacha Waruyuba	Gnr/N/6914	Chakusia Gitagama	Gnr/191217
Chata Maganga	L/Bdr/10601	Chege Mungai	Gnr/N/41414
Chepkiyeng Kibtono	Gnr/N/9854	Chibwana Lutawe	Gnr/10707
Chigulu Seoganile	Gnr/192390	Cirisomusempa	Gnr/34527
Cornall Alfons	Gnr/DT/8200	Cuthbert Maware	Bdr//7079
Cyprian Karoli	Gnr/DT/10573	Daata Busi	Gnr/L/96899
Damson Mlela	Gnr/DT/7509	Daniel Ganga	Gnr/L/11520
Dani Lutangira	Gnr/N/16535	Dankani Kalogo	Gnr/L/58438
David Mwamanyeta	Gnr/L/182695	Dominico Sylvester	Gnr/DT/7174
Dominiko Muswa	Gnr/L/51132	Domini Kabakama	Gnr/DT/8507
Edward Bokoko	Sgt/DT/7724	Edwardi Ajumi	Gnr/N/9818
Ego Kabarok	Gnr/N/11135	Eilsante Yeremia	Gnr/DT/7115
Elifraha Nhando	Gnr/DT/7118	Elukira Timeri	Gnr/24373
Enecheto Angoma	Gnr/L/59815	Enerikokamya	Gnr/34526
Enriko Moro	Gnr/L/51114	Erasto Yathiga	Gnr/L/58441
Erenyo Obong	Gnr/L/51186	Eria Kyobe	Gnr/34533
Erifazi Muwanga	Gnr/N/7285	Erinya Oyiko	Gnr/N/11533
Ernest Byalugaba	Gnr/DT/7169	Ernesti Salamba	Gnr/L/58484
Erukana Agwai	Gnr/L/51144	Ezekiel Daniel	Gnr/Ac/3407
Fabian Laurent	Gnr/DT/7419	Felician Nyamija	Gnr/DT/7168
Festo Okong	Gnr/N/6336	Fidele Olevka	L/Bdr/51117
Filipo Chilanga	Bdr/DT/7134	Francisko Bala	Gnr/L/51147
Frank Archi	Gnr/DT/9473	Fundi Rwayero	Gnr/30039
Gabriel Aroko Okelo	Gnr/L/22077	Gabriel Augustine	Gnr/DT/7636
Gabriel Saidi	Bdr/DT/7433	Gabu Auvcha	Gnr/N/11470
Gabulyeri Musoke	Gnr/34547	Gachiri Gitubi	Gnr/26671
Gandera Kitinere	Gnr/DT/7526	Gatino Ngarc	Gnr/40200
Gatira Kamau	Gnr/M/4526	Geleman Miyambi	Gnr/L/50401
George Katuta	L/Bdr/DT/7417	George Kingora	Gnr/L/52444
George Mukasa	L/Bdr/34554	Gerifas Aruta	Gnr/23625
Gidioni Atege	Gnr/L/51101	Gikonyo Gitee	Gnr/L/58356
Gimahe Masubo	Gnr/DT/10715	Girisomu Magoma	L/Bdr/L/50704
Gitau Kabuli	Bdr/9876	Gitera Mungai	Gnr/L/58679
Githumbi Thimba	Gnr/1524	Guncili Nguvumali	Gnr/L/50243
Gwakululu Mwasoni	Gnr/182955	Hamedi Kirua	Gnr/DT/8571

Hamasi Jileje	Gnr/DT/7412	Hamasi Kasell	Gnr/DT/10574
Hamasi Mwakitalu	Gnr/DT/6791	Hamasi Nangumile	Gnr/DT/7612
Harry Chitokoma	Dvr/45135	Hashim Mgoperiny	Gnr/L/50397
Hehedi Salehe	Gnr/44111	Hemedi Mlajila	Gnr/DT/7423
Hinini Sikala	Gnr/L/24521	Horry Sangolo	Gnr/46655
Hussein Mwondoma	Gnr/DT/10496	Ibrahim Defa	Gnr/L/50445
Idiki Boka	L/Bdr/34537	Ikinyan Juguka	Gnr/L/52434
Isaga Mwita	Gnr/DT/10618	Isanda-Orondo	Gnr/N/6835
Israeli Kitenga	Gnr/53968	Issa Mohamed	Gnr/L/50395
Issa Ngembano	Gnr/Dj/7431	Jakobo Andreas	Gnr/DT/8420
James Arabinfoi	Gnr/DT/7600	James Nganga	Gnr/20185
Jasoni Kibopile	Gnr/L/182257	Jekonia Odvru	Gnr/18872
Jenani Ali	Gnr/L/51166	Jerenimus Jiel	Gnr/L/30430
Jetulio Lagwe	Sgt/N/9836	Johana Sambuo	Gnr/46591
John Kaspare	Gnr/DT/10751	Joko Odokonyang	Gnr/L/51095
Jonathan Ali	Gnr/DT/7396	Jon Odihiambo	Gnr/M/1895
Josephat Katea	Gnr/L/58737	Joseph Chewe	Gnr/DT/10335
Juliano Ipele	Gnr/N/9823	Julius Masame	Gnr/DT/7617
Juma Andikisi	L/Bdr/G/1996	Juma Lihayo	L/Bdr/6109
Juma Pamba	Gnr/DT/7625	Juma Saida	Gnr/L/50472
Juma Umari	Gnr/N/14856	Kabuzu Masegese	Gnr/DT/10580
Kahagur Francis	Gnr/L/52433	Kahoi Kabubo	Gnr/L/20195
Kairori Wairumbi	Gnr/L/50053	Kalii Muoki	L/Bdr/N/6931
Kalyuki Gujiri	Gnr/L/58431	Kamau Njuguma	Gnr/L/58092
Kamawu Kaluw	Gnr/L/58430	Kamba Manyesha	Gnr/L/50424
Kamigwa Kathura	Gnr/L/18186	Karani Riua	Gnr/L/18183
Karanja Gunya	Gnr/N/6927	Karanja Kimthia	Gnr/Nr/5637
Kara Thare	Gnr/7519	Karega Magesa	L/Bdr/10657
Karioki Luthue	Gnr/L/58530	Karioki Mshidi	Gnr/Nr/5636
Karunde Kandubuka	Bdr/7553	Kasian Pius	L/Bdr/10703
Kasim Jabiri	Gnr/DT/8566	Kasindye Sinohele	Gnr/DT/10585
Kaspari Kilache	Gnr/46588	Kassim Musa	Gnr/87802
Kathuka Ndajo	Rsm/19036	Kazi Mwanankani	Gnr/DT/6156
Kazwene Mpako	Gnr/DT/10787	Keiyonga Rakaresi	Gnr/L/18635
Keli Kilu	L/Bdr/13095	Kesekya Ogwol	Gnr/L/51138
Keya Chigyta	Gnr/L/17779	Khamis Kabou	Gnr/L/50431
Khasiala Shakara	Gnr/L/52439	Kiamba Nthei	Gnr/46606
Kiangi Nzioka	Gnr/N/10086	Kibilat Gieborge	Gnr/N/11947
Kibindu Nzioka	Gnr/N/10190	Kibor Arap Tilia	Gnr/N/11678
Kibugebert Kiberen	Gnr/N/20054	Kibuti Njarguara	Gnr/28777
Kigan Chogo	Gnr/L/30766	Kigidi Mugika	Gnr/6427
Kiiyili Kiangi	Gnr/N/10209	Kilonzo Makau	L/Bdr/6928
Kilote Itumo	Bdr/N/10105	Kiluka Katama	Gnr/10684
Kilutu Mumo	Gnr/N/7007	Kimanga Mutelu	Gnr/N/10703

APPENDICES

Kimani Gaitho	Gnr/L/58345	Kimani Kikonyera	Gnr/20184
Kimanzi Kilombe	Gnr/2046	Kimau Kkwinga	Gnr/N/6903
Kimege Wambura	L/Bdr/7490	Kimela Mgunga	Gnr/DT/7557
Kimeu Kusi	Gnr/10204	Kimingi Kheya	Gnr/L/58479
Kimisha Kanga	Gnr/10696	Kimoi Keino	Gnr/11684
Kinyunya Baruti	Gnr/10610	Kipetar Boit	L/Bdr/9660
Kipole Kisolo	Gnr/N/6882	Kiprono Wabaso	L/Bdr/1929
Kiptotarap Birir	Bdr/N/724	Kireka Kabirure	Gnr/9729
Kisenge Mugekenyi	Gnr/23011	Kishiwa Malilo	Gnr/10694
Kisila Mutyeasa	Gnr/N/10074	Kitanyi Kikwaa	Gnr/N/4887
Kithome Mbobo	Gnr/N/19373	Kituto Mwambu	Gnr/29922
Kiulamagelwa	Gnr/L/96754	Kivo Matandiko	Gnr/181269
Kolonelio Osowa	Gnr/N/11455	Kolongo Kawugila	Gnr/DT/10334
Komia Kapera	Gnr/DT/7515	Korobi Mparakule	Sgt/DT/7428
Krispo Efraim	Gnr/16678	Kubira Nganera	Gnr/L/58440
Kulwa Nkune	Gnr/10785	Kuyonga Mwita	Gnr/10439
Labanson Kibuika	Gnr/L/58088	Lazaro Joseph	L/Bdr/7125
Lazaro Lucwinya	Gnr/L/51103	Ledekiah Juma	Gnr/N/22275
Leo Stanislaus	Gnr/DT/8191	Leslie Mhayaya	Gnr/DT/7634
Liandro Avuo	Gnr/L/51130	Ligi Ndotero	Gnr/DT/7127
Lombu Chuli	Bdr/Ac/23312	Lowat Ngoromai	Gnr/N/6926
Ludowiko Lutaya	Gnr/34519	Lujuo Tundu	Gnr/L/50247
Lukagu Ntamu	Gnr/34509	Lukonge William	Gnrdt/8505
Lumeleji Manaha	Gnr/L/50415	Lutebeba Apera	Gnr/L/51188
Maangi Kiluma	Gnr/13031	Mabala Masele	Gnr/DT/10584
Mabere Gimore	Gnr/DT/7480	Mabula Magele	Gnr/DT/10775
Machai Wanzofu	Bdr/1998	Machari Gachanja	Gnr L/29456
Macharia Mutisia	Gnr/N/3039	Mafuru Mboga	Gnr/DT/10658
Maganga Kabugila	Gnr/DT/10611	Maganga Kandia	Gnr/99546
Maganga Mayani	Gnr/DT/7627	Maganga Shija	Gnr/DT/10603
Mainge Ndunda	Bdr/L/12428	Maingi Nthei	Sgt/N/10089
Makala Tambi	Gnr/DT/10748	Makewa Kulu	Gnr/N/9675
Makotnga Waku	Gnr/N/6907	Makurumo Shija	Gnr/DT/10590
Malale Madinda	Gnr/DT/10587	Malilo Lugusha	Gnr/DT/10569
Malingumu Malato	Gnr/DT/7545	Malingu Tibendal	Bdr/L/50218
Mangera Masaga	Gnr/DT/10754	Manjo Sakrani	Gnr/DT/7734
Manreti Nzee	Gnr/L/11377	Marcel Komaanl	Bdr/L/51145
Mariata Ndekuonia	Gnr/182144	Mariba Muniku	Gnr/DT/10625
Mariserino Zenald	L/Bdr/13807	Marua Makwao	Gnr/DT/10666
Marunde Chuga	Gnr/DT/10564	Marwa Isore	L/Bdr/10718
Marwa Nyamatende	Gnr/DT/10731	Masala Kunwa	Gnr/L/50195
Masano Kwande	Gnr/DT/10680	Masato Manyelele	Gnr/DT/7546
Masau Waryuba	Gnr/DT/10637	Masenga Masanja	Gnr/DT/7527
Mashet Shitsukane	Gnr/33697	Masimwanda Ngula	Gnr/10786

Masubo Nsungu	Gnr/DT/10623	Matai Hailoni	L/Bdr/7729
Matata Kanyalu	Gnr/DT/10737	Matau Kinyungu	Sgt/2995
Matayo Abdallah	L/Bdr/7421	Matayo Machibya	Gnr/DT/7511
Matayo Okidi	Gnr/N/6237	Matena Ngandakwi	Gnr/43433
Mateyo Mahona	Gnr/L/50422	Mati Mukuralinda	Gnr/57456
Matiku Mwita	Gnr/DT/10768	Matoke Nyamkuja	Gnr/DT/10206
Matongo Mkole	Gnr/DT/10789	Maugu Njagi	Gnr/30342
Mawina Roweta	Gnr/53960	Mayunga Kapigawa	Gnr/10609
Masil Mashnzu	Gnr/DT/10589	Mbasa Bwiso	Gnr/DT/10630
Mbigo Mtegeta	Gnr/DT/10398	Mbogo Mdaki	Gnr/DT/10576
Mboje Mabula	Gnr/L/50237	Mbono Nzau	Gnr/Ser/9617
Mboyi Kimani	Gnr/SWR/3488	Mbugwa Wakiritu	Gnr/L/58077
Mburugo Dwalo	Gnr/L/57945	Mbuta Mulwa	Gnr/N/10088
Meineradi Mkiga	Gnr/DT/10649	Meli Mbanda	Gnr/DT/7501
Mgabu Gizaba	Gnr/DT/10650	Mganga Mgaluli	Gnr/L/181024
Mgunya Saidi	Gnr/53989	Mhanga Siraja	Gnr/L/96893
Michael Nyamba	L/Bdr/7409	Mikeri Labou	Bdr/N/423
Minaru Mwaluanda	Gnr/L/17927	M'itonga M'mboga	Gnr/L/19274
Mkondera Isiji	Gnr/L/94322	Mkwabi Kapepele	Gnr/DT/10788
Mkwaya Tugara	Gnr/DT/10632	M'naiture Naiture	Gnr/L/30874
Mohamedi Juma	Gnr/DT/8567	Mohamed Kalela	Gnr/DT/10711
Mohamed Masudi	Gnr/DT/10579	Mohamed Musa	Gnr/L/50392
Mohia Murioki	Gnr/L/58069	Mosa Seweli	Gnr/DT/10578
Mpagama Ruswaga	Gnr/DT/10743	Mrisho Kihamba	Gnr/L/50182
Mrisho Kisesa	Gnr/DT/7505	Mrisho Mhaluka	Gnr/DT/7621
M'ruk'nga Baimanene	Gnr/30880	Msabila Mlundi	Gnr/DT/7503
Msafiri Mohamedi	Gnr/L/181358	Mtambo Zahabu	Gnr/DT/6700
Mthangal Wamususa	Gnr/L/50408	Mua Kilonzi	BSM/N/1233
Mudembe Mugaduru	Gnr/L/30048	Muema Ileli	BSM/N/10106
Muinduko Maitha	Gnr/N/12015	Mukila Makau	Gnr/12054
Mukora Kabue	Gnr/27829	Mule Ndambuki	Gnr/N/10191
Muli Kioko	Sgt/L/50117	Muli Muatha	L/Bdr/N/6911
Mundui Kimaru	Gnr/L/57943	Mundu Nyakwara	Gnr/DT/10640
Mungahu Lukulu	Gnr/38515	Mungai Chege	Gnr/L/52445
Mungai Githo	Gnr/L/58315	Munyaswa Mbatha	Gnr/N/10207
Murago Ihuku	Gnr/L/58966	Murambo Musembo	Gnr/N/9688
Muromi Kitonga	Gnr/DT/10720	Murongo Odeny	Gnr/DT/10763
Musa Lupongo	Gnr/DT/7624	Musa Mutesmi	Gnr/26089
Musioka Mutinda	Bdr/3221	Musobi Votoi	Gnr/N/9689
Musya Maitha	L/Bdr/L/50141	Musyoka Ngata	Sgt/N/10704
Muteshi Etambo	Gnr/SP/23624	Muthoka Etumo	Gnr/N/10233
Mutio Mylitu	Gnr/N/6899	Mutiso Kithia	Gnr/N/3972
Mutiso Mzumbi	Gnr/N/14826	Mutua Katunda	Gnr/N/10098
Mutua Mmethiya	Gnr/N/10104	Mutuku Kioko	Gnr/N/16451

Muwili Sianda	Gnr/3531	Muya Kasyoka	Gnr/N/14724
Muya Kikueo	Gnr/N/4709	Mwandi Nyangazi	Gnr/L/50402
Mwangi Macharia	Gnr/L/58528	Mwaniki Karani	Gnr/Swr/4553
Mwanzia Nindi	Gnr/N/3398	Mwawela Noanga	Gnr/DT/6464
Mwenda Karuiki	Gnr/L/58318	Mwinyikheri Zohoro	Gnr/51764
Mwita Chacha	Gnr/DT/7496	Mwita Makabrutya	Gnr/DT/7641
Mwita Marwa	Gnr/DT/7498	Mwita Marwa	Gnr/DT/10627
Mwita Wisandara	Gnr/DT/10661	Mworia Njuguna	Gnr/L/58375
Nafukho Werere	Bdr/G/3410	Naliuma Bwana	Gnr/N/6933
Nasanaire Manasi	Gnr/L/51159	Nasoro Mtwale	Gnr/DT/10646
Nazarus Amri	Gnr/DT/7402	Ndambile Mihambo	Gnr/DT/10593
Nderu Mbaki	Gnr/L/58976	Nd'angio Ndenyaku	Gnr/L/78815
Ndeto Mukuna	Gnr/2539	Ndolo Ndundo	Gnr/80946
Ndoo Ileli	Gnr/N/10084	Ndooni Muthoka	Gnr/8299
Ngaeji Mfaume	Gnr/L/182084	Nganda Ndumbi	L/Bdr/6810
Ngichuru Mibuwa	Gnr/N/3014	Ngochi Unyangi	Gnr/20194
Ngual Otieno	Gnr/7969	Ngugi Gathanwa	Gnr/L/52442
Ngui Musia	Gnr/N/10095	Njagara Rwita	Gnr/18190
Njoroge Kamau	Gnr/L/29945	Njoroge Kamau	Gnr/L/58432
Njoroge Nganga	Gnr/L/18088	Njoroge Njuguna	Gnr/N/42098
Njuguna Chege	Gnr/L/58313	Njuguna Kabubu	Gnr/L/58526
Nthenge Nziuko	Gnr/N/10696	Nyabosa Wiriba	Gnr/DT/7456
Nyaburuti Waduru	Gnr/DT/10717	Nyadera Adhiambo	Gnr/15622
Nyambori Mangera	Gnr/DT/10104	Nyamlinga Ngasa	Gnr/DT/10572
Nyangoko Kibisa	Gnr/DT/10643	Nyawade Agutu	Gnr/L/5344
Nyelu Handi	Gnr/DT/10597	Nyoukumo Mwita	Gnr/DT/10207
Nzile Machiya	Gnr/L/50236	Obayi Ojewa	Gnr/DT/10724
Obel Oluoch	Gnr/L/52438	Obuya Sienya	Gnr/L/11519
Ochang Omenya	Gnr/N/11737	Ocheyi Oganga	Gnr/50199
Ochieng Meso	L/Bdr/11648	Ocieng Tundo	Gnr/N/6997
Odera Odinga	Bdr/N/10711	Odera Muhowa	Gnr/14819
Odiera Okaka	Gnr/N/11819	Odiyo Ndede	Gnr/N/40799
Odongo Nyakado	Gnr/L/5290	Odongo Okello	Gnr/N/11847
Ogutu Ulyechi	L/Bdr/DT/7533	Ohito Nyambare	Gnr/G/1741
Ojuok Ogutu	Gnr/G/1790	Okambo Abong	Gnr/N/6985
Okanyi Asala	Gnr/46659	Oluga Ojuong	Gnr/36783
Oluoch Okutima	Gnr/40063	Omari Abdallah	Gnr/DT/7601
Omari Hassani	Gnr/DT/9491	Omari Salim	Gnr/DT/6701
Omari Selemani	Gnr/L/50390	Omongo Ogira	Gnr/28984
Onyuna Otieno	Gnr/G/1732	Osuru Ochen	Gnr/N/11404
Otera Okoli	Gnr/37149	Otieno Oliech	Gnr/L/20183
Otile Alele	Gnr/N/11911	Ouna Abiya	Gnr/N/7000
Owala Oodhiambo	Gnr/L/30984	Owichi Kiraryo	Gnr/DT/7452
Owuko Olewe	Gnr/57867	Pafula Matobu	Gnr/L/14779

Patrick Akwilapo	Gnr/DT/9633	Paul Gitau Kamau	Gnr/L/20685
Paul Kibiko	Gnr/1467	Paulo Baitwanasa	Gnr/L/59711
Paulo Makonda	Gnr/DT/10769	Paund Pauli	Gnr/DT/7192
Penco Robi	Gnr/DT/10663	Petero Okok	Gnr/OO/6896
Petero Oradi	Gnr/L/18946	Petero Serumaga	Gnr/L/50537
Petro Zacharia	Gnr/DT/7535	Phillipu Abdallah	Gnr/DT/7424
Pinga Kitundu	Gnr/DT/10679	Rajabu Faraji	Gnr/L/50227
Rajabu Salehe	Gnr/L/50403	Ramadan Ibrahim	Gnr/L/50448
Ramadhani Dikala	Gnr/DT/10408	Ramad Kabarazy	Gnr/DT/10745
Ramadhani Salehe	Gnr/L/50228	Ramazan Asumani	Gnr/DT/7513
Ramaz Mhondogwa	Gnr/DT/10339	Rams Wakalukwa	Gnr/DT/7721
Rashidi Tibanyange	Gnr/L/50211	Richard Omoulo	Gnr/L/58401
Richard Opiyo	Gnr/L/58529	Rioba Mwita	L/Bdr/10626
Roderck Mukhama	Gnr/L/53885	Rukiko Katiriko	Gnr/DT/10660
Rukwaro Kimondo	Gnr/L/17712	Ruto Kaino	Gnr/N/11136
Ruziga Mapolu	Gnr/DT/10738	Sabastian Mikaeli	Gnr/DT/8442
Saida Abdurahmani	Gnr/DT/7530	Saidi Bakari	Gnr/L/92271
Saidi Kanduru	Gnr/DT/7610	Saidi Mayumani	Gnr/L/50391
Saidi Sengenge	Gnr/DT/8570	Saidi Tibanyenda	Gnr/L/50221
Salenge Malugu	Gnr/31776	Salim Ali	L/Bdr/DT/740
Salumu Bakari	Gnr/L/50178	Salu Mwandi	Bdr/N/6918
Samuel Pande	Gnr/L/29533	Samwiri Butada	L/Bdr/22403
Sandago Karuguru	Gnr/DT/7516	Sanifolo Mabunga	Gnr/10418
Sasamula Mtima	Gnr/DT/10749	Sebast'n Semandia	Gnr/DT/7629
Selemani Mzee	Bsm/DT/7622	Selestin Modest	Gnr/DT/7103
Shabani Mbaraku	Bsm/L/50425	Shabani Ramazon	Gnr/L/50420
Shabani Selemani	Gnr/23547	Shabani Wambali	Gnr/L/50188
Shabula Khamasi	Gnr/L/30067	Shangiru Mungare	Gnr/DT/10734
Shija Kayanda	Gnr/DT/7518	Shija Kurwa	Gnr/DT/7131
Shija Mapigi	Gnr/DT/7529	Shilala Saida	Gnr/L/50471
Shimba Masele	Gnr/L/50239	Shindy Thunyana	Gnr/L/58696
Siaford Lembaranga	Gnr/Oo/9174	Sila Arum	Gnr/DT/7640
Silanda Panda	Gnr/DT/10248	Siligwi Mwita	BSM/DT/7576
Sinare Makiloli	Gnr/L/90370	Singe Mutubu	Gnr/KML/3478
Sitefano Kamya	Gnr/L/51104	Sitina Masiba	Gnr/DT/10642
Sondo Onyango	Gnr/DT/10665	Stainer Kamtunda	Bdr/DT/7565
Stanley Bulwad	Gnr/M/7420	Stephano Muhina	Gnr/DT/9638
Stephano Shimba	Gnr/L/50208	Sultan Silver	Gnr/DT/8564
Sumaili Mohamed	Gnr/DT/10695	Sunga Masamaki	Gnr/L/50214
Suter Kisut	Sgt/N/9849	Tairifa Kabitira	Gnr/L/78732
Tajishe Mwalyoyo	L/Bdr/7730	Takhagasi Moshi	Gnr/L/58142
Thomas Nambela	Gnr/DN/17980	Thomas Obare	L/Bdr/7484
Thomas Oyoo	Gnr/L/29263	Tiginya Maloja	Gnr/L/50412
Titu Kyusia	Gnr/N/10798	Tiyuba Wambura	Gnr/DT/10762

Uduba Opiyo	Gnr/N/11594	Usheleka Kulyama	Gnr/DT/10567
Valentino Lungene	Gnr/L/51136	Valtino Okeny	Gnr/L/51094
Victor Mlungusye	L/Bdr/7608	Virsino Owor	Gnr/N/7757
Wainana	Gnr/L/58658	Wakaba Yethuka	Gnr/L/57944
Waliekere Bwtala	Gnr/L/29275	Walter Aw'thogol	Gnr/46643
Wambua Maingi	L/Bdr/10193	Wambua Masila	Gnr/N/7037
Wambugu Mbaki	Gnr/L/31030	Wambura Kwame	Gnr/DT/10670
Wani Kenyi	Gnr/N/9798	Wanseobosa	Gnr/20985
Warire Muneria	Gnr/G/3061	Warungu Wande	Gnr/Ser/9618
Waryuba Sieki	Gnr/DT/10730	Wasikpyo Bunde	Gnr/L/29865
Waweru Kamau	Gnr/L/52436	Wawiru Munya	Gnr/26060
Were Oyo	Gnr/L/58522	Wickson Fulaye	Gnr/L/53754
William Matiku	Gnr/DT/10634	William Matovu	Gnr/17113
William Raban	Gnr/DT/6790	Williamu Andiku	Gnr/N/11469
Wilson Okumu	Gnr/N/6660	Wisaka Kitaguti	Gnr/DT/10624
Wiyama Mutaka	Gnr/L/20191	Yakobo Mmeingiya	Gnr/DT/7618
Yakobo Musoke	Gnr/34516	Yeremia Ngollalei	Gnr/DT/7124
Yoa Mwenkkusho	Bdr/DT/7611	Yohana Ambali	Bdr/DT/7411
Yohana Asteri	Gnr/DT/7166	Yohana Mshsa	Bdr/DT/7432
Yohanes Sewga	Gnr/DT/7393	Yokana Kiwanuka	Gnr/20981
Yowana Musoke	Gnr/49600	Yozefu Bamweyana	Gnr/L/51112
Yozefu Bitambaki	Gnr/51221	Yozefu Sikitonko	Gnr/L/51167
Yuiya Mulili	Gnr/N/6938	Yusuf Ngozi	L/Bdr/DT/7626
Yusuf Bakale	Gnr/R/23627	Zacharia Odoi	L/Bdr/L/51115
Zakaliya Oyat	Gnr/N/9843	Zakaria Mikael	Gnr/DT/7150
Zedekiya Kayondo	Gnr/Ut/27	Zeruba Nsubugia	Gnr/L/57295
Zubert Juma	Gnr/DT/7632		

56 (Uganda) Bty. (301st Regt)

Marona Sang	Gnr/11688	Ndongori Muma	Bdr/G/3060
Shikanga Wanjala	BSM/G/3055		

57 Bty. (301st Field Regt)

Lufunyo Asikuliya	Gnr/DT/7728	Michael Wanzofu	Gnr/G/1990

East African Electrical and Mechanical Engineers

Cedrick Kenneth	Crftn/45175	China Matewere	Crftn/45131
Chipazi Chipiza	Crftn/27315	Daniel Jumbe	Pte/45300
Eleck Chibwana	Pte/45214	Erifasi Onyango	Pte/51228
Frachshon Malikeba	Pte/54177	Francis Mungura	Cpl/20205

Grayson Sitima	Pte/54289	Isaac Thomu	Crftn /45186
James Chasoloka	Pte/45008	Lailo Julius	Pte/45238
Morris Samiti	Crftn /45290	Muhia Karaja	Crftn /190325
Mwaka Suba	Pte/26692	Ndalu Kisala	Pte/N/10814
Record Sadi	Crftn/45179		

East African Corps of Signals, 11th East African Div. Sigs

Benedicto Kasirye	Sign/N/16515	Francis Musoke	Sign/N/14981
Kamau Musa	Sign/N/12337	Kisagi Mwambeo	Sign/N/14851
Maina Kibata	Sign/N/16494	Muse Musyoni	Sign/15548
Paul Arare	Sign/00/6903	Peter Karamagi	Sign/N/16531
Taricisio Otto	Sign/N/16562	Were Wambulwa	Sign/L/18793
Wilhelm Joseph	Sign/DT/9463		

E.A.A.S.C

Robertson Chikoya	Dvr/45368

Total East African personnel lost 675

APPENDIX 4

NAMES OF OTHER KNOWN PERSONNEL MISSING

Ship's Company

R. W. M. Whiteman DSC	Captain	Albert R. Anderson	Chief Steward
(Roderick William Macaulay)		Arthur Mitchell	Purser
Leonard Arnold Lowe	3rd Officer	George P. C. Monie	Assistant Purser
William Allan	Chief Engineer	Stanley Townsend	Canteen Steward
Frederick Simons	2nd Engineer	A. Hong (Chinese)	Carpenter
James Docherty	3rd Engineer	A. Jong (Chinese)	Carpenter
Thomas C. Paterson	4th Engineer	Albert Edwin Burley	Storekeeper
John Corbett Hall	Junior Engineer	Leslie Walter Lewis	Troopkeeper
Horace Terence Jordan	Junior Engineer	Dr Rotherham	Sick Bay
Charles Kidd	Junior Engineer	C. A. Sing (Chinese)	Fitter
Sidney Cubitt M. Patrick	1st Rad. Officer	Dr F.G. Adye-Curran	Surgeon

Indian Crew: Medical Orderlies

Abdul Qadir	Cassab	Mubarak Ali	Cassab
Mukdal Rahman	Seacunny	Qudrat Ali	Seacunny

Indian Crew: Engine Room

Abdul Ali	Trimmer	Abdul Karim	Oiler
Amir Husain	Trimmer	Arzumand Ali	Fireman
Desa Cruz Francis P.	Storekeeper's Mate	Faiz Ahmad	Fireman
Farnuz Ali	Trimmer	Firoz Ali	Lamp Trimmer
Joynal Aradin	Donkeyman	Lobo Antonio	Storekeeper
Monterio Antonio	Storekeeper	Mozam Khan	Trimmer
Munu Mian	Oiler	Muzaffar Ali	Oiler
Nazir Ahmad	Oiler	Sabed Ali	Trimmer
Sarar Ali	Fireman	Sayid Ali	Oiler
Shams-Ul-Haq	Fireman	Shamsur Ali	Trimmer
Sultan Ahmad	Fireman	Tufail Ahmad	Fireman

Tufail Ahmad	Oiler	Vigas Presentace C.	Storekeeper
Wali Mian	Fireman		

Indian Crew: Deck Department

Abdul Aziz	Seaman	Abdul Bari	Deck Serang
Abdul Husain	Seaman	Abdul Khair	Seaman
Abdullah	Seaman	Abdul Nabi	Tindal
Ahmad Rahman	Seaman	Ali Ahmad	Seaman
Alim Bakhsh	Tindal	Ali Mian	Seaman
Amir Ahmad	Seaman	Anu Mian	Seaman
Britto Alfonso	Boy	Faiz Ahmad	Seaman
Habib-Ur-Rahman	Winchman	Khalil-Ur-Rahman	Seaman
Mubasar Ali	Tindal	Mufiz Ullah	Seaman
Muhammad Mian	Seaman	Muhammad Nawaz	Seaman
Mukhtiar Husain	Seaman	Munir Ahmad	Seaman
Nazir Ahmad	Seaman	Nur Ahmad	Seaman
Nur-Uz-Zaman	Seaman	Sadiq Ahmad	Seaman
Sahkur	Bhandary	Samir-Ud-Din	Seaman
Sheikh Abd'l Halim	Seaman	Sheikh Badshah	Bhandary's Mate
Siraj-Ul-Haq	Seaman	Thanda Mian	Seaman
Tobarak Shiekh	Seaman	Wilayat Ali	Seaman
Yaqub Ali	Seaman	Yunis Mian	Seaman

Indian Crew: Saloon Department

Alfonso Abel Manoel	General Servant	Antao Anthony	General Servant
Azavedo Joao Camil	General Servant	Baretto J. Salvadore	Butcher
Bhagwan	Topass	Chhote Lal	Topass
Correa Pascal	General Servant	Crasto Louis	General Servant
D'costa Antario M.	General Servant	De Costa Victorino	Topass
Dias Domingo M.	Pantryman	Dias Joaquim Manoel	Asst Butcher
Dias Salvadore	Topass	D'souza Bernard	Pantryman
D'souza Casmir	Cook	D'souza Francis	Topass
D'souza Gabriel	General Servant	D'souza Jerome	General Servant
D'souza John	General Servant	D'souza John	Boy
D'souza Ladros	Baker's Mate	D'souza Pascoal	Butcher
D'souza Sanon	Assistant Baker	Fernandes Bernardo	General Servant
Fernandes Castadio	Iceman	Fernandes Douglas	Assistant Baker
Fernandes Fulgacio	General Servant	Fernandes Joaquim	General Servant
Fernandes Louis	Cook	Fernandes Manuel	General Servant
Fernandes Minguel	Pantryman	Fernandes Roque F.	General Servant
Fernandes Sebastiaô	Cook	Ferrao Antonio S.	General Servant
Furtado Jose Sebastio	Assistant Cook	Furtado Pedro M.	Topass

APPENDICES

Furado Simon	Pantryman	Gama Baptisto	Assistant Cook
Gama Ramad	Cook	Gomes A.J. (63 years)	Baker (oldest)
Gomes Domingo F.	General Servant	Gomes Mariano	General Servant
Gonsalves Salvadore	Assistant Cook	Kalakatti	Topass
Kaslu	Topass	Laslado Ladru	Scullion
Marcial Gonsalinha	Topass	Marquis Floriano	General Servant
Martins Augostina	General Servant	Mathias Vincent	Butcher's Mate
Menzies Thomas	General Servant	Miranda Joseph P.	Chief Cook
Monterio John	Iceman	Munir Ahmad	Iceman
Oliveira Raphael	General Servant	Pereira Alexio P.	Assistant Baker
Pereira Felix	General Servant	Pereira Valentine	General Servant
Pinto Antonio	Butler	Pinto Lawrence	Cook
Pinto Pascoal	General Servant	Pinto Robert	General Servant
Pires Caetan	Butcher's Mate	Rocha Antonio	Topass
Rodrigues Pelegrino	General Servant	Rodrigues Remedio	Assistant Cook
Rodrigues Sebastio M.	Cook	Sanchis Louis	Baker's Mate
Tauro Ellias	General Servant	Vaz Caeton Francis	General Servant

Total Ship's Crew lost 156

Maritime Royal Artillery Gunners (DEMS)

NAME	REGT/NUMBER	NAME	REGT/NUMBER
Clayden S. G.	2ndMar/5830180	Dowsett K.	2ndMar/1476760
Shimmin W. D.	4thMar/3864572	Sparrow	5thMar/5119681

Total Gunners lost 4

Women's Royal Naval Service

Barden Jeanette Lilian	3rd Officer	Batten Hazel Mary	Wren/N/68311
Breakell Marie E.	Wren/M/39735	Carlyle Agnes Kyle	Wren/40911
Dalton Winifred Beach	Ldg/Wren	Dean Cicely Coppard	3rd Officer
Fletcher Gladys	L/Wren/D/9426	Hunter Ethel M.	Wren/43624
Nickson Aileen Audrey	Wren/N/38215	Nye Beatrice M.	Wren/N/46151
Robinson Marion Carson	3rd Officer	Smail Heather M.	Wren/R/43136
Stafford Audrey Hilda	Wren/60199	Todd Margaret P.	Wren/N /51125
Valentine Helen Morag	L/Wren/P/21962	White Betty Ramsay	Wren/R/36211
Wylie Pamela Irene	L/Wren/N/47044		

Total Wrens lost 17

PASSAGE TO DESTINY

Royal Naval Officers

Bunt Richard Ford	Lieutenant	Merrill Leslie	Surgeon Lt Cmdr
Mickleburgh L.	Wrnt Writer Off (S/Afr)	Toomey P. J.	Wrnt Sply Off
Whitelaw R.	Pymstr Lt Cmdr (Rnvr)		

Royal Navy (including 7 DEMS)

NOTE: The Prefix letters, shown below, denote where each Naval Rating was originally registered. C = Chatham (Chats), D = Devonport (Guzz), P = Portsmouth (Pompey) and L = Lowestoft

NAME	RANK/NUMBER	NAME	RANK/NUMBER
Addis Cyril W. C.	St2Cl/P/Kx121419	Allcock Albert E.	St2Cl/D/Kx524747
Allen Arthur C.	Ordsig/D/Jx575731	Andrews Cyril	Ab/P/Jx334765
Arliss Reginald F.	Po/D/J105903	Ashton Edward	Ech/C/Mx621236
Astbury Sidney	Dems/Ab/D/Jx398234	Baker Ivor Lewis	T2Cl/D/Kx553594
Banks James	Ab/D/Ssx22054	Barker Robert H.	Odsigc/Jx350669
Barnicoat Harry	Po/D/J 39129	Barrett Frank J.	Ab/C/Jx311077
Bennett Norman	Mech/C/Mx622410	Bicknell Kenneth	Odsig/C/Jx571853
Bingham S. C.	Omech/C/Mx622947	Binns Geoffrey	Odcdrc/Jx609074
Birch Ronald Roy	Era5Cl/P/Mx503123	Birch Stanley	Erm/P/Mx117134
Blake John H.	Erm/C/Mx 95127	Bleasby Frank	Astd/D/Lx572948
Blencowe Eric J.	St2Cl/D/Kx527840	Bowden A.	T2Cl/D/Kx163128
Bower Maurice F.	St1Cl/P/Kx137967	Brackell William	T2Cl/D/Kx560488
Bracknell W. A.	St2Cl/D/Kx560488	Bradshaw S.	Odsigc/Jx455080
Bratt Victor E.	St1Cl/C/Kx126541	Burgoyne R. W.	Era/C/Mx622849
Burt Albert Leslie	Lairm/Faa/Fx91604	Butler Clifford	T1Cl/D/Kx134698
Carpenter R. D.	St1Cl/C/Kx127792	Carter Gordon E.	Mec/D/Mx510964
Clark Reginald A.	Omech/P/Mx 98882	Clark William	Ab/C/Jx315436
Clarke Edward A.	Erm/P/Mx 98988	Clarke Harold	T2Cl/D/Kx527719
Cockle Arthur G.	St2Cl/D/Kx157935	Cole Stanley W.	Era5/P/Mx501954
Colley Harold J.	Sba/D/Mx100773	Cooke Leonard E.	Lwrtr/C/Mx 86810
Cooksey R. A.	Sba/D/Mx100202	Cookson John E.	Pom/C/Mx125945
Cooper Roland	Joiner/P/Mx635914	Cope Mark	Erm/P/Mx500090
Cousins Walter	Mech/D/Mx560490	Crease Reg A.	Ordtelc/Jx572048
Creaser Edward	Telghst/P/Jx357194	Crowther C.	Era/D/Mx509466
Davies Robert H.	St2Cl/D/Kx161459	Davy George W.	Sba/C/Mx112357
Deane Frank W.	Erm/P/Mx 99001	Devlin Hugh	St2Cl/P/Kx106598
Diamond Bryan L.	St1Cl/D/Kx135429	Dill David	Chmecp/Mx96678
Dolan Joseph	Sba/D/Mx150403	Dolce Leslie	Sba/D/Mx100617
Donlon Patrick M.	St2Cl/D/Kx566249	Dudley John D.	Asckd/Mx533786
Edmonds E. G.	Erm/P/Mx124438	Edwards William	Sba/D/Mx100690
Entwhistle D.	Sba/D/Mx100691	Ewing Peter S.	2Cl/D/Mx560168

APPENDICES

Farrell John J.	St2Cl/D/Kx560427	French N. W.	Erm/P/Mx502259
Fluin Bernard F.	St2Cl/D/Kx161094	Gaffney Peter	Astwc/Lx604427
Galley William	Po/Ck/Rnvr/238904	Gifford George	Odteld/Jx405720
Gilby Daniel B.	Cpo/D/J 18858	Godfrey W. A.	Hprt/C/Mx620621
Goodway Stanley	Ordsmn/D/Jx424270	Gouge William G.	Sast/D/Mx614821
Graham Charles	St2Cl/D/Kx560170	Gumbrell Dennis	T2Cl/D/Kx527880
Hammerton A.	Sba/C/Mx111950	Hanshaw Ronald	Ab/C/Jx396607
Harding John S.	Mech/C/Mx622591	Harris William	Ab/C/Jx255311
Harrison Cecil H.	St1Cl/D/Kx137877	Harrison J. F.	T2Cl/D/Kx528032
Hartley Alan H.	Sba/C/Mx112060	Harvey B. F.	Ordteld/Jx405170
Hassan James W.	Mech/C/Mx621199	Henbest Roy	Ordtelp/Jx453801
Henry Joseph J.	Erm/C/Mx507222	Hilliar Gilbert H.	Sba/D/Mx100694
Hillman Ronald	Mech/C/Mx620510	Hogg Duncan M.	Ab/D/Ssx29792
Holloway J.	Erm/P/Mx500966	Horton Arthur W.	Po/C/J111627
Housley Derek C.	Sba/C/Mx112056	How Henry George	Omecc/Mx703481
Howlett George	St2Cl/D/Kx596088	Hubbard William	Ordteld/Jx405109
Hudson Kenneth	Ordtel/D/Jx405110	Humphreys G.	T2Cl/D/Kx528054
Hunter Geoffrey	Ordtel/D/Jx405579	Jefferies Henry C.	Ech/D/Mx649134
Jones Albert	Mech/C/Mx105431	Jones Albert	Ech/D/Mx534700
Jones Richard	Mec/D/Mx520970	Kelly Dermot Paul	Ab/D/Ssx33432
Kenyon James V.	St2Cl/D/Kx527895	Kirkham Kenneth	Ech/C/Mx621201
Kingston Ronald	Telghstp/Jx370565	Laming Jack Philip	Asckc/Mx576645
Laytham Richard	Lsmn/P/Jx226142	Lea Stanley Bertin	Ech/C/Mx622431
Leader Frederick	Skbthpo/C/X8014	Le Gassick Fred	Ech/D/Mx510974
Lloyd Leonard	St2Cl/D/Kx553486	Lucas Arthur W.	Ph/Faa/Jx223754
Macey Edward G.	St1Cl/D/Kx145460	Matthews T.J.	T2Cl/D/Kx554126
Mcewen Llewellyn	Erm/P/Mx117707	Mcgillivray T	Ook/C/Mx110326
Mckenzie James P.	St2Cl/D/Kx527782	Middlebrooke P.	St2Cl/P/Kx634623
Mills Kenneth	St2Cl/D/Kx527908	Milne James	T2Cl/D/Kx527788
Moore James W.A.	St/Lt/Jx130992	Morley Andrew	Odcdrd/Jx609091
Moss Eric Henry	St/1Cl/D/Kx161688	Moulding Arthur	T1Cl/D/Kx135303
Muir Daniel	Rnvr/154161	Muir Thomas Guinea	
			St2Cl/D/Kx512661
Murdock Edward	St1Cl/D/Kx161692	Newman Chris	Mec/C/Mx621206
Newnham Eric C.	Mec/D/Mx511087	Newns Frederick	Erm/C/Mx506669
Nichols Stanley	Mech/C/Mx621474	Noble Leslic	T2Cl/D/Kx527919
Oates Kenneth	Sba/P/Mx 94451	Oldham Albert	Ech/D/Mx511087
Pearce Percy E.	St1Cl/P/Kx134165	Pengilly Sidney	Ech/C/Mx621207
Pinckard Gilbert	Steward/C/Lx577350	Platt Gordon D.	Ech/C/Mx622600
Pratt William J.	St2Cl/D/Kx528046	Pullin Geoffrey	Sba/P/Mx111806
Punch Maurice C.	Mech/C/Mx622600	Quinn John E.	Ab/D/Jx346072
Rate Leslie Ewart	Erm/P/Mx124436	Redman Frederick	T1Cl/D/Kx145124
Reed Adam T.	Sba/P/Mx111820	Richards William	T2Cl/D/Kx527671
Richardson John	Ldgsmn/C/Ssx24291	Rigby Thomas H.	Ab/P/Jx249931

127

Roden Thomas S.	Ldstk/C/Kx 93932	Rooke George W.H.	Ab/D/Jx150493
Ross Edward Ewen	St2Cl/D/Kx527796	Ruby Fergus John	T2Cl/D/Kx562920
Scott Arthur	St2Cl/D/Kx527804	Sexton Sydney O.	Ech/C/Mx507932
Shaw Donald	Ab/P/Jx209886	Skelly Thomas J.	T1Cl/D/Kx161288
Smith Douglas	Ab/P/Jx167352	Smith Jack	St1Cl/P/Kx 94559
Southgate A.	Omech/C/Mx 26046	Spencer Michael	T2Cl/D/Kx562917
Stobbs Leslie	St2Cl/D/Kx553631	Stoneham R.	Erm/P/Mx501066
Stroud Albert W.	St2Cl/D/Kx528082	Stuart Frederick	Sba/D/Mx 90614
Thomas Noel	Asstwdc/Lx 31232	Thompson N.	Mec/D/Mx311089
Thompson Robert	Po/D/Jx152250	Thorne K. G.	T2Cl/D/Kx527945
Thornsby P. A.	Splyas/P/Mx614517	Todd Albert Talbot	St1Cl/D/Kx 93317
Townsend John	Ldgsmn/C/Jx351062	Tunney Norman	Ook/P/Mx121065
Turner Alfonso P.	Po/D/J108036	Tyrer George A.M.	Mec/D/Mx511094
Uff William Henry	Ordcdr/P/Jx573922	Vaughan David	T2Cl/D/Kx527951
Wall Arthur	Stpo/C/Kx 83396	Waller Percy F.	T2Cl/D/Kx527955
Walsh William J.	St2Cl/D/Kx527692	Watson David T.T.	Po/C/Ssx12916
Weightman A.	Mec/D/Mx511090	Weston Charles E.	T1Cl/D/Kx141060
Wheatley George	Mech/C/Mx622440	White David	Erm/P/Mx126001
White William T.J.	Sigmn/Lt/Ssx26487	Whitehall S.	T2Cl/D/Kx527564
Whiteman Joseph	Ab/D/Jx303556	Whittle Arthur	T1Cl/D/Kx161299
Wilkes Henry	St1Cl/D/Kx117043	Williams Noah	Ech/D/Mx511028
Winter Oliver J.J.	St2Cl/D/Kx527961	Wood George F.	Po/D/Mx510804
Woods John	St/Patsvc/Lt/X10530S	Woodward A.C.	T2Cl/D/Kx527823
Yeo William James	St2Cl/D/Kx527702	Yeuell Claude T.	Suasp/Mx578335

Royal Navy on loan from HMS *Hawkins*

Dempster Alan K.J.	Lsgmn/P/Ssx27646	Soskaug Leslie	Sgm/Safr74773V

Royal Australian Navy (RNR)

Daunt Terence	Ab/S 4322	Sidey John	Ab/S 4994
Thornton Rex	Ab/S 5197	Williams D.	Ldgsmn/22033

Royal Marines

Newman George	Boybgler/Ch/X 3867	Perry Joseph	Marine/P/X106094

Total Royal Naval Personnel lost 226

Women's Territorial Service (East Africa) Ex.FANY (EA)

Austin Barbara Mary	Sgt/K/541	Calisher Anne	Cpl/K/570
Camerer Constance H.	Sgt/K/180	Hook Sonia	Sgt/K/113

Kentish Barbara	Sgt/K/200	Moojen Florence Fairburn	Sgt/K/253
Thompson Beatrice Dunbar	Sgt/K/233	Le Poer Trench Patricia H.	Sgt/K/188

Total W.T.S. Lost 8

East African Military Nursing Service
(* denotes Queen Alexandra's Imperial Military Nursing Service)

Airey Freda	Sister/*260226	Arnott Constance	Sisteredcc/359
Atkin Joyce Kathleen	Sister/*270574	Barwell G. M.	Sister/Edcc/360
Bateman Edith Mary	Sister/*257776	Beecher Grace	Sister/Edcc/359
Brown Amy	Sister/*274633	Burrows Isabella	Sister/*266663
Cashmore Patricia	Sister/Edcc/371	Clark-Wilson J. M.	Sister/Edcc/362
Dalgarno Elsie Alice	Sister/*208105	Dann Elizabeth D.	Sister/*250095
Davies Margaret E.	Sister/*238669	Dervan Gertrude	Sister/*266750
Dewar Alice W.	Sister/*270637	Dowling Beatrice O.	Sister/*266662
Dryden Clara Martha	Sister/——	Farrelly Mary	Sister/*274735
Fitzgerald Catherine	Sister/*274636	Harvey Grace W.	Sister/*274658
Hastings Valerie F.	Sister/*263805	Humphrey Muriel C.	Sister/*274079
Ievers Eileen Mary E.	Matron/*206235	Jarman Marie	Sister/*274755
Johnston Maud F.	Sister/*274737	Kells Maggie Jane	Sister/*274727
Kells Winifred E.	Sister/*274733	Leckey Muriel Emily	Sister/*208615
Leech Barbara E.	Sister/*266730	Littleton Mary J.	Sister/*236448
Maclaren Jean Noel	Sister/*238130	Mcmillan Marion L.	Sister/*266937
Moore Isabella	Sister/*215107	Morgan Sarah	Sister/*274164
Nuttall Phyllis	Sister/*274639	Pirie Barbara	Sister/*274846
Richardson Sybil G.	Sister/*206418	Robertson Helen M.	Sister/*274402
Senior Doris Ena	Sister/*260544	Smith Marjorie	Sister/*260546
Spence Isobel	Sister/*274753	Taylor Katherine M.	Sister/*266464
Thomas Jane Mair G.	Sister/*270493	Urquhart Mary A.	Sister/*274611
Walker Kathleen H.	Sister/*266754	Warwick Roberta	Sister/*266463
Whitaker Mafalda S.	Sister/*274344	White Gwendoline M.	Sister/*274074
Willis Annie Amelia	Sister/*209648	Wolseley-Lewis A.	Sister/Edcc/363
Young Eleanor Jane	Sister*274629		

Total Nursing Staff lost 51

Royal Artillery, attd. 301st Field Regt. East African Artillery

Allen Aubrey	Sgt/962646	Allen William	Gnr/14358464
Apted Leslie	L/Bdr/1089341	Archer Stanley W.	L/Sgt/957433
Ashforth Levi A.	Sgt/1606690	Ayscough Ray	Gnr/14390789
Bamforth Geoffrey	Gnr/14329931	Barclay Henry	Gnr/3196373
Barden Cecil James	Sgt/6397328	Barratt Percy D.	Gnr/14285139

Bartle Frank	Gnr/14369465	Bellinger Edward	Bqms/904532
Boaz Harold	Rsm/794758	Boldison George	Sgt/806940
Booton Norman	L/Sgt/965838	Boyd Joseph Markey	Bdr/1093839
Boyes Alfred	L/Bdr/1079794	Braithwaite R.	Bdr/6141635
Breen Patrick J.	Sgt/836524	Bridger Alec Ernest	Sgt/1077223
Bromley Fred Henry	Gnr/14259449	Brown Donald Olley	Sgt/833319
Brown Harry	Gnr/14379678	Buckles Henry	L/Bdr14310937
Bullock Cyril	Gnr/14355185	Carpenter S.F.G.	Sgt/823048
Carr William George	Gnr/14271609	Casey James	Gnr/1785972
Cave Terence Charles	Sgt/1550698	Chamberlain J.	L/Bdr/940857
Chappell Ernest William	Gnr/14271774	Clark Edward M.	L/Sgt/950010
Cleary John	Sgt/819314	Collingwood J. F.	Gnr/14309607
Connaughton J. M. F.	Capt/117507	Copsey George	L/Bdr14283946
Cowie Robert	L/Sgt/891083	Cranshaw Arthur	L/Sgt/897158
Croydon Peter Charles	Capt/165480	Crump Cyril	Gnr/14552781
Cutler John Edward H.	Gnr/2082094	Daniels Eric George	Sgt/807260
Dare William Henry	Sgt/1072138	Dearing Ernest	Gnr/325021
Deavin Gerald	Capt/207361	Dickinson Harold	Gnr/14551001
Donoghue Charles	Gnr/14551003	Dunster Sydney	Bdr/7894344
Earey Raymond John	Gnr/14310611	Elliott Eric Allen	Gnr/14302697
England Samuel Francis	Bdr/848885	Faircloth Edward J.	Gnr/14546913
Feeney Martin	Sgt/860764	Fisher Jack	Gnr/14513021
Forsyth John	Sgt/922019	Friend Leslie John	Bdr/1156237
Frost Leslie John	Sgt/831643	Geary Adam	L/Sgt/854155
Gibbard Edwin George	Bdr/1152668	Goddard Thomas	Gnr/1500107
Grantham George A.	Bdr/1061001	Green Walter William	Gnr/1152876
Griffiths William S.	Sgt/872260	Hardy Frank Arthur	L/Sgt/820409
Harker John	Lieut/153539	Hatton Frank E.	Sgt/791738
Haynes Herbert Leslie	Gnr/14315813	Head Henry Graham	Major/100918
Hewitt Kenneth Percy	Sgt/885991	Hird Eric	Bdr/1141250
Hislop John Bain	Sgt/951073	Hoad Edward Arthur	Bdr/1122569
Holden Archibald James	Sgt/1131209	Hoptrough Basil J.	Gnr/14331358
Humphries William G.	Gnr/14342040	Hutchings Frank	Bsm/1072496
Jenvey Frederick Arthur	Sgt/899290	Jones George	Gnr/14267757
Jones James	Bdr/930933	Keet James	Gnr/14305525
Lacey William	Bdr/1118345	Lambert Cyril T.	Gnr/14337820
Lasham Ronald	Bdr/981755	Leahy William Henry	Bdr/14512344
Leddington Leslie A.	Sgt/1086716	Lennie Thomas	Gnr/14503926
Lenton Ralph Percy	Capt/214748	Lewis Edward	Sgt/983657
Longstaff Leslie C.	Gnr/14267536	Lucas Anthony J.	Bdr/865790
Lunn Albert	Gnr/959192	Macarthur A.	Gnr/14297116
Mcgregor William	L/Bdr/819143	Mckenzie Kenneth	Capt/100373
Mclaren Frank William	Sgt/852137	Mcnab Andrew	Sgt/870507
Manning Albert H.	Bdr/940081	Manton Robert G.	Bdr/872839

Martinelli Clement A.	Sgt/966600	Mason Aubrey C.	Gnr/14545305
May Cyril Hubert	Gnr/1112914	Milward Jack	Bqms/892637
Mitchell Peter Horn	Sgt/917198	Moore Edgar Cyril	Bdr/1142928
Moore Thomas Charles	Bqms/724920	Moores John Henry	Bdr/779786
Murkett Alfred George	Sgt/769745	Natham Trevor A.	Lieut/174821
Nichol James Carse	L/Cpl/2571231	Nile Harry Archer	Gnr/14274738
Norris Edward William	Bdr/947754	North William Ernest	Gnr/6353927
Owen Thomas John	Bsm/853978	Pettigrew Herbert	Sgt/875663
Preston Philip S.	Capt/187185	Regan George R.	Sgt/811704
Reynolds Jonathan C.	Gnr/14546956	Riddett John Ernest	Bdr/1135975
Robertson Stanley E.	Gnr/14299482	Rowberry Henry J.	L/Bdr/1155047
Russell Timothy Main	Gnr/1749371	Sanders Ivor Ernest	Bdr/876275
Savill George Thomas	Gnr/1757480	Sewell Albert James	L/Bdr/1156249
Sharpley Roger	Major/92224	Shaw Alfred	Sgt/913105
Shilofsky Hyman	Gnr/5193006	Simkins Harry	Gnr/14506157
Smith Harry	Bsm/1072024	Starkey Edmund J.	Sgt/977026
Titcomb Frank	Gnr/14277372	Waite Joseph N.	Gnr/14320219
Wallace R.W.	Bsm/820577	Walmsley James	Bsm/400459
Walter Jack	L/Bdr/1145600	Warren John A.	Gnr/6354177
Warwick William	Gnr/924774	Watson Edward	Gnr/14323477
Weaver Wallace	Gnr/14267777	Weekes Sidney E.	Gnr/1746537
Weller Harold	Gnr/1764932	White Arthur V.	Gnr/918707
Wood Frank W.	Gnr/2160737		

56 Btn. (301st Regt)

Downie Robert Gordon	Rsm/X45

Army – General List

Aggett Hudson Boyce	Major/322300

Royal Electrical and Mechanical Engineers (REME)

Boswall Sidney Walter	Cpl/5439708	Colley Charles S.	Cpl/3306422
Dunwoody Alexander	Lieut/291290	Edwards Patrick B.	Cpl/7589727
Fielding James A.	Sgt/198532	Futcher Herbert V.	Cpl/10565425
Hamilton Robert M.	Cpl/10564370	Lewis Richard D.	Cpl/161091
Matthews S.	Sgt/199752	Ross Roderick	Qms/7598317
Smith William Norman	Cpl/904919	Taplay Sidney G.	Cpl/6851859

Kenya Regt. attd. East African Artillery

Percival P.B.	Sgt/Lf/3103	White G.M.	Sgt/Lf/3058

East African Electrical and Mechanical Engineers

Fittall L.A.W.   Sgt/B/407

Army Catering Corps

De Courcy Harold   Sgt/6397177

Royal Army Medical Corps (RAMC)

Farrimond Leslie	Pte/7382261	Florentine Lawrence H.	Pte/7383558
Odell Samuel Arthur	Pte/7399361	Pelling George Frederick	Sgt/7359262
Rotheram Ewan B.	Major/119626	Toghill Herbert Charles	Pte/7398993

Royal Corps of Signals, 11th East African Div. Sigs

Connelly Michael	Cpl/2342436	Emery Francis Patrick	Cpl/2325293
Hamerton William	Sgt/2323019	Harrison Philip	Cpl/2336473
Norman Harold	Cpl/5885336	Spence Kenneth H.	Cpl/2336233
Wood Francis E.	Cpl/2587595		

Total Army personnel lost 174

Civilians

Mrs Merrill Beryl Elsie   Master Merrill Anthony David
Mr Gandar-Dower Kenneth Cecil   (5 Months)
(War Correspondent)

Total Civilians lost 3

Total personnel (of European/Asian/Oriental origin) lost 622
Total East Africans lost 675
Total personnel on board at time of sinking 1,511
Total rescued 214
Total number lost (on Saturday 12th February 1944) 1,297 people

APPENDIX 5

SECOND WORLD WAR ALLIED MERCHANT NAVY DISASTERS

17th June 1940 the SS *Lancastria* (16,243 tons) sank whilst preparing to leave the French port of St Nazaire. From a total complement of 5,000 British military personnel and 310 crew members, 2,833 perished when the liner was bombed by German Junkers 87 (Stuka) bombers. Time taken to sink, 30 minutes. Chances of survival 47%.

12th September 1942 the SS *Laconia* (19,695 tons) was torpedoed by U-*156*, commanded by Werner Hartenstein, NNW of Ascension Island in the South Atlantic. From 463 officers and crew, 286 military personnel, 80 civilians (mainly women and children), 1,793 Italian prisoners of war and 103 Polish guards totalling 2,725 people, 1,614 perished. Time taken to sink, 73 minutes. Chances of survival 41%.

12th February 1944 the SS *Khedive Ismail* (7,513 tons) was torpedoed by the Japanese U-Boat *I-27* commanded by Toshiaki Fukumura. From a total complement of 1,511 personnel, 1,297 people perished. Time taken to sink, under 2 minutes. Chances of survival 14%.

Although the *Khedive Ismail* incident was the worst Allied disaster involving servicewomen in any war, to date (for no fewer than seventy-six female personnel perished on that fateful day) it may be of some interest to readers to contrast this with other Second World War incidents involving women. (Note: None are listed during the evacuation of Singapore, although there were some Australian Army nurses sunk whilst escaping on the *Vyner Brooke*. Twenty-two nurses who survived her sinking were captured along with some soldiers and subsequently shot, in the back, by the Japanese. Only one nurse survived, by feigning death after being shot in the loin whilst waist-high in the water.) There were other incidents during the evacuation, again including nursing staff, on the *Kuala, Empire Star* and *Tanjong Penang*.

Below are listed, in order of occurrence, ships lost with women in the services, onboard:

17th October 1939, SS *Yorkshire* (10,184 tons) owned by Bibby Line, sunk by U-*37* at 44° 52´N 14° 31´W. Fifty-eight perished including one WTS.

19th August 1941, SS *Aguila* (3,255 tons) owned by Yeoward Bros., sunk by U-*201* at 49° 23´N 17° 56´W. Eighty-nine perished including twenty Wrens.

27th October 1942, MV *Stentor* (6,148 tons) owned by A. Holt and Co., sunk by U-*509* at 29° 13´N 20° 53´W. Forty-four perished including four Nursing Sisters.

6th December 1942, SS *Ceramic* (18,713 tons) owned by Shaw Saville & Albion, sunk by U-*515* at 40° 30´N 40° 20´W (estimated). Six hundred and fifty-five perished including twenty-three Nursing Sisters (only one male person survived).

24th January 1944, SS *St. David* (2,702 tons) OHMS Hospital Carrier, bombed by aircraft at 41° 10´N 20° 53´W. Fifty-seven perished including two Nursing Sisters.

Total (not including the *Khedive Ismail* incident) 50

APPENDIX 6

NOMINAL LIST OF SURVIVORS RECORDED
ON HMS *PETARD*

Royal Artillery, attd. 301st Field Regiment, East African Artillery

Addinson A.P.	Sgt/803552	Blackwood M.H.	Captain
Bool C.K.	Captain	Boucher A.J.	Sgtac/1462779
Bracken W.H.	Gnr/2038636	Clow R.H.	Bdr/1133050
Davis G.B.R.	Capt	Dewitt E.	L/Bdr/996670
Evemy A.	Gnr/14283956	Fenton W.	Bsm/781411
Gale J.U.	Capt	Gilhay D.	Gnr/14255078
Green W.	Bdr/4465110	Groom H.	L/Sgt/909291
Hepworth	Bsm/805735	Jefferies G.E.	Lieutenant
Meacher	Gnr/1156494	Mole A.G.W.	Bsm/832727
Owens C.	Lt/Qm	Peake A.J.	Sgt/826315
Power W.M.	Sgt/Ac/1065184	Roden F.	Gnr/14247216
Routledge W.	Gnr/14269079	Thornton J.R.	Bdr/768819
Smith A.H.	Gnr/13054528	Smith L.N.	L/Sgt/906976
Stevens J.A.	Lt/ Col	Waterfield	Bdr/1456397
Wheeler	L/Bdr/14285252	Williams C.F.	Bsm/953527

301st Field Regiment. East African Artillery

Abisai	Gnr/Sig/DT/10746	Adina	P/St/L/31081
Aeunda	Fitter/190598	Alamani	Sgt/4371
Alban	Sigmn/DT/10710	Allegro	Dvr/22429
Alexander	Sigmn/38397	Ambcge	P/St/L/57941
Amiri	Sigmn/DT/8446	Amon	Sigmn/DT/7723
Andrea	Dvr/5384	Asangalwiye	Sigmn/DT/7720
Attilio	Sgt/L/51161	Bachubira	Dvr/L/50222
Abu Bakari	Sigmn/DT/7162	Bakari	Gnr/DT/7420
Barnabas	Gnr/DT/7426	Bashi	Gnr/L/50439
Basingo	Gnr/5052	Beato	Gnr/DT/10706
Bene	L/Bdr/DT/10708	Bernard	P/St/L/58080
Blassio	L/Cpl/12342	Boniface	Sigmn/DT/7416

Buonaventuad	Sigmn/DT/7138	Burugu	P/St/L/58527
Celestini	Sigmn/DT/8443	Chanu	Dvr/5010
Chesuluk	L/Bdr/2450	Chuli	Armasst/190083
Clementi	Dvr/L/50400	Cristofa	P/St/182238
Damiano	Dvr/11460	Daniel	Gnr/Sig/L/50538
Doto	Dvr/L/50225	Elige	Sigmn/N/11926
Enos	Sigmn/DT/7563	Emanuel	P/St/183124
Fidenzio	Gnr/Sig/DT/10507	Geramija	Gnr/DT/10780
Hatimu	Swper/DT/18191	Hoja	Sgt/DT/7637
Idi	Cook/DT/10336	Ionatius	Dresser/3530
Isaac	Gnr/Sig/DT/7564	Issa Yakub	Gnr/L/50430
Jacob	Sigmn/DT/7130	Kaloke	Blksmth/6082
Kamabela	Gnr/DT/13929	Kaman	P/St/29904
Kanau Mwangi	P/St/29336	Karaja	Mess Ck/29878
Kasamu	Gnr/10133	Kasimbagi	Gnr/10565
Kea	Sigmn/43353	Khaima	Gnr/DT/7418
Kinwaga	Gnr/DT/10375	Kipkeri	L/Bdr/DT/11717
Kiposke	Dvr/DT/11145	Kitchi	Gnr/DT/8566
Kwami	Gnr/L/50421	Libarus	Sgt/Bdr/1067
Livingstone	L/Cpl/DT/16609	Lusania	Clerk/L/51097
Mabugu	Dvr/DT/10782	Magaga	Gnr/DT/10667
Maiki	Dvr/DT/10774	Martino	Gnr/L/51722
Masalu	Cook/L/50203	Masan	Bdr/DT/11700
Mathiku	Sigmndt/10566	Mbowe	Gnr/DT/10723
Mganga	Gnr/DT/7524	Michael	Gnr/DT/10713
Moher	P/St/502347	Mohogemtu	Gnr/DT/10602
Kamau Mpeya	P/St/L/50072	Muhani	Gnr/DT/7025
Musa	Bdr/Ut/57	Mwargi	Messstdl/58291
Mwrura	P/St/20190	Mwaruwambara	Gnr/96769
Mzugwa	Gnr/DT/10771	Nampwan	Gnr/DT/7427
Nasodo	Gnr/DT/10702	Ngalua	Dvr/L/50205
Ngioki	Dvr/3647	Ntulile	Gnr/DT/10081
Nyona	Elect/L/51713	Oburya	Gnr/21988
Pantaleo	Dvr/DT/11323	Rashidi Ali	Gnr/DT/10374
Rashidi	Sigmn/6798	Rashwea	Sigmn/2385
Robert	Sigmn/22243	Robin	Sigmn/L/53375
Saidi	Dvr/DT/10617	Sampson	Gnr/L/51165
Samuel	P/St/L/58346	Sedini	Gnr/DT/7061
Shaluk	Dvr/45113	Sidrek	Dvr/4528
Sija	Gnr/DT/10606	Simeon	Dvr/L/51190
Thomasi	P/St/L/52441	Wambua	Bdr/DT/10212
Wilson	Gnr/L/51093	Yampanda	Gnr/DT/10604
Yasini	Gnr/Sig/DT/7635	Yegela	Gnr/DT/10777
Yohanna	P/Sgt/20192	Yusuf	Sigmn/DT/16552

APPENDICES

Zuberi	Fitter/46876

Total Army personnel rescued 143

Women's Territorial Service (East Africa) – formerly of FANY

West Gloria	L/Cpl/K/641

Women's Royal Naval Service

Chessell D.J.	Wren/45456	Munro Norah	L/Wren/59023

150th General Hospital

Garrett M.	Sister/——	Hutchinson Phylis	Sister/——
Meredith-Clease	Sister/P 266352		

Total number of female personnel rescued 6

HMT *Khedive Ismail*

Ainslie John T.	3rd Radio Officer	Duncan John	Chief Officer
Leleu R.I.	Troop Officer	Mawlan W.	Electrician
Munday Cecil H.A.	2nd Officer	Thompson William	2nd Radio Officer

Deck Crew

Ali Jacob	Suckunnie	Gufur Abdul	Bhandarrie
Hussein Jayu	Tindal	Ismail Mohamel	Barber
Junal Anwarad	Kalassie	Kadir Abdul	Kalassie
Shufeil Mahomed	Suckunnie		

Engine Room Crew

Ali Ayul	Fireman	Ali Musufur	Serang
Bish Roy	Fireman	Hormia Ali	Trimmer

Saloon Crew

Fermandes Andrew	Scullion	Fermandez Eric X.	Troop Veg. Cook
Fernandez Eric	G.S. Boy	Mendes Manuel	Troop Veg. Cook
Vas M.F.	Troop Storekeeper		

Total number of *Khedive Ismail*'s crew rescued 22

Royal Naval Personnel

Barlow L.	Sba/C/Mx112072	Bowles C.	St2Cl/D/Kx161367
Bowles S.	St2Cl /D/Kx 157261	Boyle P.T.	Surgeon Lt. Rnvr
Bridges E.G.W.	St2Cl/D/Kx 527345	Briggs W.	Po/Mecp/Mx116991
Brunner R.H.	Lt. Rn	Casey W.	St1Cl/D/Kx105121
Cockerell R.	Erm/P/Mx 99575	Cox V.A.	L/Mecd/Mx 510966
Crabb Percival	Stokerpo/D/Kx 85084	Currie K.	St2Cl/D/Kx 560419
Davis A.	O/Tel/P/Jx 405921	Daykin K.	L/Mechc/Mx125308
Docwra L.T.	Marine/P/X 3183	Field F.	St2Cl/D/Kx 528027
Fox Tom B.	C/Coder/C/Jx 609705	Green H.S.	Lt (Sp) Rnvr
Green S.F.	Po/C/Ssx 20055	Griffiths T.	St2Cl/D/Kx 526565
Hack F.	Photo(A)/Jx 453857	Halloway D.T.	Era4/C/Mx 53957
Heath R.	Tel/D/Jx 453159	Hodkison R.	St2Cl/D/Kx527882
Howard William	Leading Signalman/P/Ssx 35227 (on loan from HMS *Hawkins*)		
Howkey B.R.	St2Cl/D/Kx 161103	Johnston A.A.	Pay Lt. Rnvr
Jordan C.	Ab/P/Ssx 29472	Mitchell H.	O/Mech /J 100764
Morgan S.	Po/D/Jx 126143	Ozanno F.C.	St2Cl/D/Kx 577310
Page W.A.	Sb Po/C/Mx 85262	Palmer J.R.	Erm/C/Mx 505902
Parry H.	Sba/P/Mx 311640	Pini P.N.	St2Cl/W2490Rah
Redman G.H.	Shipwrt/P/Mx 61594	Rudd S.	Erm/C/Mx 62271
Smith J.J.P.	Ab/P/Jx 157004	Storr L.	Ab/R 142770
Turner Edwin W.	Osigmn/P/Jx 573375	Turner L.C.	Po/D/Jx 137854
Walker A.	Po/D/J 115090	White G.	Ldg Smn/C/J 44739

Total number of Royal Naval personnel rescued 43
Total number of survivors rescued – 214

APPENDIX 7

SIGNALS

SIGNALS SENT TO AND FROM KHEDIVE ISMAIL AND HM SHIPS APPERTAINING TO ZIG-ZAG DECISIONS 9th–12th FEBRUARY 1944

No 1. From Captain Whiteman (*Khedive Ismail*) to Captain Josselyn (HMS *Hawkins*), 0814/9th. [local times are used throughout this appendix unless otherwise specified]

I am afraid we shall not be able to save daylight on the 13th. SS *Varsova* is doing her utmost speed at present. I estimate the speed of the convoy to be currently 11.2 knots and it will require 13.5 knots to save daylight. Suggest our ETA/Colombo will be 0800/14th. What do you think?

No 2. From Captain Josselyn to Captain Whiteman. 0907/9th.

Your 0814. Agree we cannot hope to save daylight and also that we should try to arrive 0800 local time. But this means an average of 12.5 knots and I am afraid we will have to zig-zag during daytime from about the 11th. I make speed through water over 13 knots but think we have a 2 knot set against us. Perhaps we may get set with us later. I hope so.

No 3. From Captain Whiteman to Captain Josselyn. 1235/9th.

If you think it will be necessary for the convoy to zig-zag, I propose that diagrams 12 and 38 are alternately used, commencing with No 12 and so on. Do you agree?

No 4. From Captain Josselyn to Captain Whiteman. 1237/9th.

I entirely agree.

No 5. From Captain Whiteman to Captain Josselyn. 0840/10th.

According to my current chart and previous voyages, we should have been enjoying a favourable set for the last two days. Instead, we have had an adverse set practically all the way. It may turn out in our favour approaching the [One and a Half Degree] Channel, at least I hope so.

No 6. From Captain Josselyn to Captain Whiteman. 0851/10th.

Your 0840. Fully agree with adverse set, but have small hope of favourable current to come. I hope that I am wrong.

No 7. From Captain Josselyn to Commanding Officer Egan (HMS *Petard*). 1001/11th.

We have had a 2 to 3 knot set against us since Monday, 7th, and I would think we were going to be luckier soon. What sets did you experience to and from Addu Atoll? [NOTE: HM Destroyers, *Paladin* and *Petard,* were still on their way to convoy KR8 and did not arrive until early the next morning, the 12th.]

No 8. From Commanding Officer Egan to Captain Josselyn. 1235/11th.

Your 1001. Local set near Addu Atoll is northerly, otherwise 1 to 2 knots westerly, my regrets.

No 9. From Captain Josselyn to Captain Whiteman. 1618/11th.

We ought to start zig-zag tomorrow, Saturday, but with zig-zag and adverse current we may not have daylight on 14th. This would mean spending a night hanging about in a dangerous area which would have to be weighed against the safety gained from the zig-zag. I think we should wait till morning stars tomorrow Saturday, before deciding.

No 10. From Captain Whiteman to Captain Josselyn. 1625/11th.

Your 1618. I quite agree.

No 11. From Captain Whiteman to Captain Josselyn. 0745/12th.

If zig-zag was omitted and commenced at dawn tomorrow Sunday, we could save daylight on the 14th. I estimate the speed overground from p.m. observed at 12.3 knots. What do you think?

No 12. From Captain Josselyn to Captain Whiteman. 0854/12th.

Your 0745. Yes, I feel we cannot afford to zig-zag yet, though the one and a half degree channel is an obvious haunt for a U-boat. Let us reconsider the matter at dawn tomorrow.

No 13. From Captain Josselyn to Commanding Officer Egan. 0859/12th.

After discussion with Captain Whiteman we have decided not to zig-zag at present. With zig-zag we are unlikely to save daylight on 14th and hanging about for a night is less preferable than no zig-zag. We are going to reconsider it tomorrow morning. What are your views?

No 14. From Commanding Officer Egan to Captain Josselyn. 1015/12th.

Your 0859. Fully concur. Restricted zig-zag only serves to wobble the jelly, anyhow! I will keep destroyers zig-zagging broadly on either side.

Author's Note:

Although the Admiralty were quite willing to blame the escort's Senior Officer – Captain Josselyn RN – for the exclusion of zig-zagging in Convoy KR8, it can be clearly seen in the above records that the main concern (of both Captains) was for the convoy's safety in view of the retention caused by unfavourable prevalent currents that persisted throughout the voyage. Both Captains Whiteman and Josselyn had discussed the feasibilities from the 9th February onwards and became increasingly alarmed at the possibilities of spending an extra night at sea in potentially dangerous waters around the vicinity of Colombo. The fact that the decision may have been a factor in the loss of so many lives is very easy to assume with hindsight.

SIGNALS MADE ON 12th FEBRUARY 1944

Six short blasts.		1434 FG.
Black pendant.		1434 FG.
Cone point up over red flag (signal for U-boat contact).		1434½ FG.
Petard from *Paladin*.	Contact doubtful. R/T.	TOD/1450 FG.
Paladin from *Petard*.	Contact Port. R/T.	TOR/1455 FG.
Paladin from *Hawkins*.	Immediate. Join *Petard* and hunt. Rejoin by dusk. TOO/1451FG. Light. P/L.	TOR/1455 FG.
Flag H at dip.		1456 FG.
Flag H close up.		1456½ FG.
Flag H dipped.		1457 FG.
Paladin from *Petard*.	Submarine is under survivors. Light. P/L.	TOR/1500 FG.
Flag H close up.		1501 FG.
Flag H dipped.		1502 FG.
Petard from *Paladin*.	Possible submarine. Light. P/L.	TOD/1504 FG.

Petard from *Paladin.*	It will be 5 minutes before another pattern is ready. Am allowing charges to subside before going in again.	
	1512 FG. Light. P/L.	TOD/1514 FG.
Paladin from *Petard.*	Are you in contact. Light. P/L.	TOR/1519 FG.
Petard from *Paladin.*	Reply No. Suspect submarine to be one mile on my starboard beam. Light. P/L.	TOD/1521 FG.
Petard from *Paladin.*	Am returning to scene now.	
	TOO/1524 FG. Light. P/L.	TOD/1525 FG.
Paladin from *Petard.*	Pass signals by R/T. Light. P/L.	TOR/1526 FG.
Petard from *Paladin.*	No contact. R/T.	TOD/1530 FG.
Paladin from *Petard.*	Join me. R/T.	TOR/1531 FG.
Petard from *Paladin.*	Shall I drop whaler with doctor to pick up survivors. R/T.	TOD/1535 FG.
Paladin from *Petard.*	Pick up survivors. R/T.	TOD/1536 FG.
Petard from *Paladin.*	Intend to ram. R/T.	TOD/1621 FG.
Paladin from *Petard.*	Do not ram. R/T.	TOD/1625 FG.
Petard from *Paladin.*	Have damaged myself. Regret after magazine flooded while trying to avoid ramming. R/T.	
		TOD/1630 FG.
Paladin from *Petard.*	Cease fire. R/T and Flags.	TOR1632 FG.
Petard from *Paladin.*	No power onboard. W/T out of action. R/T.	
		TOD/1639 FG.
Colombo W/T from *Paladin.*	*Hawkins'* 12th/0905 Z. Submarine surfaced. Am engaging with gunfire and depth charges. My position 088 KBYY 18. TOO/12th/1115 Z. W/T. 3290 Kc/s. Fleet Code.	TOD/1122 Z.
Commander in Chief Eastern Fleet from *Hawkins*	*Khedive Ismail* torpedoed and sunk in position 0 degrees 57 minutes North. 72 degrees 16 minutes East.	TOO/12th/0905 Z.
Petard from *Paladin.*	Gearing room, engine room and tiller flat flooded. Still have steam. Am working steam ejectors and hand pumps, and am ditching topweight. Damage was done by bow of submarine when I altered to port, to try to avoid ramming.	
	TOO/1746 FG. Light. P/L.	TOD/1648 FG.
Paladin from *Petard.*	Cease fire. R/T.TOD/1719 FG.	
Petard from *Paladin.*	Am unable to steam. Could you tow us from alongside so that your pumps can be used. Tiller flat is not flooded. TOO/1721 FG. R/T.	
		TOD/1729 FG.

APPENDICES

Colombo W/T from *Paladin*.	My 12th/1115 Z. Japanese submarine blown up. TOO/12th/1155 Z. W/T. 3290 Kc/s. Fleet Code. TOD/1200 Z.
Paladin from *Petard*	Close down set watch on VHF. Channel 'A'. R/T. TOR/1628 FG
Commander in Chief Eastern Fleet etc. from *Petard*.	Japanese submarine torpedoed. Position 01 degrees 05 minutes North 72 degrees 22 minutes East. TOO/12th/1822 FG. Naval Cypher 'A'. TOR/1832 FG.

Abbreviations used:

underlining = Greenwich Mean Time

FG	Foreign GMT or Local Time.
Kc/s	Kilocycles.
Light	Method of sending message – Aldis Lamp.
P/L	Plain Language.
TOD	Time Of Despatch.
TOO	Time Of Origin.
TOR	Time Of Receipt.
R/T	RadioTransmission (talking to one another via microphone/headset).
VHF	Very High Frequency.
W/T	Wireless Transmission (Morse Code).
Z	GMT (Greenwich Mean Time).

APPENDIX 8

MESSAGES CONCERNING THE MYSTERIOUS JAPANESE SURVIVOR

ADM 199/2052   SECRET   13th February 1944

U-boat incident report No 1604 Re 8924 after torpedoing of SS *Khedive Ismail* at 0905Z/12th in 00° 57´ N 72° 16´ E. The U-boat (Japanese) was attacked with gunfire and by ramming of U-boat, one survivor from U-boat recovered by HMS *Petard*.

Signed V. J. Van Der Byl.

ADM 199/2289   MOST SECRET
WAR DIARIES SUMMARIES REPORTS
February 1st – 15th, 1944. Volume 159.

East Indies convoy KR8 attacked, U-boat sunk. 8(a) SS *Khedive Ismail* in convoy KR8 was torpedoed by a Japanese U-boat at 0905Z today and sank in less than 2 minutes in 00° 57´ N 72° 16´ E. (about 100 miles NNW of Addu Atoll). *Petard* picked up 200 survivors out of a total of 1,497 passengers and crew. (b) *Paladin* and *Petard* which, with the cruiser *Hawkins,* constituted the escort of KR8., attacked the U-boat when it surfaced an hour later, and after a running fight *Paladin* rammed U-boat and *Petard* finally destroyed it by a torpedo hit, in 01° 25´ N 72° 22´ E. *Paladin* was damaged by ramming the U-boat and was taken in tow by *Petard* for Addu Atoll. One survivor of the U-boat was picked up.

WAR DIARY – 12th February 1944.

Saturday KR8 *Khedive Ismail* sunk. U-boat sunk. *Paladin* damaged. *Khedive Ismail* torpedoed and sunk in 00° 57´ N 72° 16´ E.

(*Hawkins* 120905Z Commander in Chief Eastern Fleet. 121101Z to all concerned).

Reference *Hawkins* 120905Z – Submarine surfaced and engaging by gunfire and depth charges 01° 25´ N 72° 18´ E. My 121115, Japanese submarine blown up.

APPENDICES

No 1 and 2 Summary of formers.

1. Ships and aircraft being sent to assist in rescuing survivors, *Paladin* damaged in collision with U-boat. Engine room, gear room and after magazine flooded and taken in tow. My present course and speed 01° 00´ N 72° 22´ E. Course 075° at 10 knots, have 200 survivors from *Khedive Ismail*. One survivor from submarine, am remaining with convoy.

2. *Petard* has 200 survivors. Ship sank in 2 minutes.

3. The surface anti-submarine escort is being sent, propose to leave convoy to reach *Petard* at dawn and transfer tow. *Petard* to rejoin convoy. *Paladin* in danger of sinking and proceeding to Addu Atoll. My P.C. and S. [Position, Course and Speed] 00° 51´ N 72° 10´ E. Course 160°, 8 knots. ETA [Estimated Time of Arrival] 0600Z 13th. Request portable pumps may be sent. Have all the survivors from *Khedive Ismail* and half of *Paladin* Ship's Company on board *Petard*. *Petard* 121600Z to C. in C.E.F. Japanese submarine torpedoed in position 01° 05´ N 72° 22´ E. Message from *Hawkins* to *Petard* – do you require assistance with survivors? If so, I will join you.

ADM 199/2289	WAR DIARY	U-BOAT CAMPAIGN
		Tuesday 15/2/1944

No 8. *Paladin* engaged Japanese U-boat with gunfire and depth-charges at 1155Z/12th in 01° 25´ N 72° 22´ E. U-boat blew up and one survivor was picked up.

APPENDIX 9

DAILY U-BOAT DISPOSITIONS BROADCAST
BY C-IN-C EASTERN FLEET

February 8th

Area G. No further news of Japanese U-boats indicated by D/F but may be in area. Scale of air escort Y.   08/0348

February 9th

No further information. No changes in scale of air escort except Area G reduced to X.   09/0324

February 10th

A, B, C, D and G. No fresh information.   10/0328

February 11th

Area G. No further information of U-boat in this area but scale of air escort remains.   11/0401

February 12th

A, B, D, E and G. No fresh information. No change in scale air escort.   12/0335

Notes: Convoy KR8 was just inside Area G when attacked. Air escort scale X indicates 'Position not entirely clear but probably no immediate threat'.

APPENDIX 10
TIME AND INFORMATION CONCERNING ATTACKS ON JAPANESE U-BOAT

HMS *Paladin* using asdic type 128A.

1st Attack
09.06 GMT. 10 charges dropped. 50-100 feet settings. Echo pitch – no doppler. Attacking speed 18 knots.

2nd Attack
09.12 GMT. 5 charges dropped. 100-200 feet settings. Echo pitch – moderate high. Attacking speed 18 knots.

3rd Attack
09.19 GMT. 1 charge dropped. 150 feet setting. Attacking speed 18 knots.

4th Attack
09.27 GMT. 10 charges dropped. 200 feet settings. Echo pitch – low. Attacking speed 18 knots.

5th Attack
09.32 GMT. 9 charges dropped. 200 feet settings. Echo pitch – moderate high. Submarine possibly blowing. Attacking speed 18 knots.

Attack on Surfaced U-boat.
Depth of water – 2,018 fathoms (12,108 feet).
Weapons used – 4", Pom Pom, Oerlikon and depth charges.
No. of rounds fired – 70.
Hits observed – 6 on base of conning tower and 3 on the bow.
Range obtained by estimation.
Type of shells used – High Explosive and Delayed Action.

HMS *Petard* using asdic type 128A.

1st Attack
09.18 GMT. No pattern fired. Attacking speed 15 knots.

2nd Attack
09.30 GMT. 7 charges dropped. 230 feet settings. Echo pitch moderate low. Little movement of target. Attacking speed 18 knots.

3rd Attack
09.35 GMT. 8 charges dropped. 300 feet settings. Echo pitch moderate slight high. Target moving right course 310°. Attacking speed 18 knots.

4th Attack

09.43 GMT. 9 charges dropped. 300 feet settings. Echo pitch slight high. Target moving slowly left turning to port. Attacking speed 18 knots.

Attack on Surfaced U-boat.

Depth of water – 2,000 fathoms (12,000 feet).

Weapons used – 4", Pom Pom, Oerlikon, depth charges and torpedoes.

No. of rounds fired – 374.

Hits observed – Penetrated conning tower and casing, burst on pressure hull, causing considerable damage to upper works.

Range obtained by estimation.

Type of shells used – high explosive (HE) and semi-armour piercing (SAP).

Range on opening fire – 1,800 feet.

U-boat surfaced, damaged at 10.50 GMT.

U-boat sunk by 7th torpedo at 11.53 GMT.

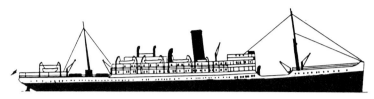

PICTURE CREDITS

1. Percival Crabb (Buster) 1915–91 photographed in his Chief Petty Officer's uniform in 1944, *author's collection* (frontispiece).
2. SS *Aconcagua*, in about the mid 1920s, *courtesy of Glasgow University* (p. 4).
3. Stern view of the *Aconcagua*, again in the mid 1920s, *courtesy of Glasgow University* (p. 5).
4. SS *Khedive Ismail* steaming out of the River Clyde, 17th April 1935, *courtesy of Glasgow University* (p. 8).
5. Side profile showing off her pleasing shape, 17th April 1935, *courtesy of Glasgow University* (p. 9).
6. SS *Khedive Ismail* entering the Grand Harbour, Malta, 31st March 1939, on one of her scheduled runs from Alexandria. Her funnel was painted bottle-green with a black top, *courtesy of Michael Cassar, Malta* (p. 10).
7. Another view, taken on the same afternoon, showing the liner turning to port prior to dropping her anchors before coming astern to her regular berth, just inside the Grand Harbour entrance below the Upper Barracca Gardens viewing area, *courtesy of Michael Cassar, Malta* (p. 11).
8. Her sister ship, SS *Mohamed Ali El-Kebir,* berthed stern-first between SS *Arandora Star* and the Italian SS *Città di Trieste,* beside the St Barbara Bastion, Malta (none of these ships survived the War), *courtesy of Michael Cassar, Malta* (p. 12).
9. Advertisement displayed, in 1939, in one of Malta's daily newspapers, showing the schedule of both ships, *courtesy of Michael Cassar, Malta* (p. 13).
10. Buster (in the wheelchair) recovering from a broken leg – 87th General Hospital, Nairobi, *author's collection* (p. 16).
11. Buster dressed and ready to join the SS *Khedive Ismail* – February 3rd 1944, *author's collection* (p. 17).
12. Route of convoy KR8, *by Brian Crabb for Paul Watkins Publishing* (p. 28).
13. The 9,800 ton cruiser HMS *Hawkins* in 1942, built in 1917, *courtesy of the National Maritime Museum, London* (p. 30).
14. The SS *City of Paris*, built in 1922 for Ellerman's Indian and South African Services. She originally had accommodation for 250 passengers, *courtesy of Glasgow University* (p. 30).
15. An aerial view of SS *City of Paris* passing the impressive coastline of Cape Town at speed, *courtesy of Glasgow University* (p. 31).

35. The anti-submarine destroyer HMS *Petard*. She joined the Eastern Fleet in January 1943, *courtesy of the Imperial War Museum, London* (p. 73).
36. Plan showing the estimated positions of the sinking of both the *Khedive Ismail* and the Japanese submarine *I-27* in relation to the One and Half Degree Channel, *by Brian Crabb for Paul Watkins Publishing* (p. 74).
37. Tracking chart of HM Ships *Paladin* and *Petard* and the estimated track of Japanese submarine *I-27, by Brian Crabb for Paul Watkins Publishing* (p. 75).
38. Some of the survivors on board HMS *Petard, courtesy of the Royal Navy Submarine Museum, Gosport* (p. 76).
39. The Special Order which was circulated to all Units of the 11th East African Division stationed in Ceylon, *courtesy of Gloria Smith* (p. 80).
40. Cliff Horrell, SS *Varsova,* gunner and one of the key eye-witnesses to the sinking of the troopship *Khedive Ismail, supplied by himself* (p. 102).
41–2. Gloria Smith (*née* West). Photographed on 25th July 1943 and more recently on the Great Wall of China, *supplied by herself* (p. 104).
43. Buster with his wife Vera in the summer of 1982, *author's collection* (p. 105).
44. Bill Howard at Bob and Maureen Macaire's home in Taplow, after being interviewed on Saturday, 3rd September 1994, *author's collection* (p. 106).
45. Dan Docwra relaxing in his home after the author had met him in August 1994, *author's collection* (p. 107).
46. Eddie Turner at his home in Torrington, North Devon, in May 1996, *author's collection* (p. 108).
47. Typed letter sent to Mrs Fox, *courtesy of Tom Fox* (p. 108).
48. Form 100 B-2, sent to Mrs Breen, *courtesy of the late Patrick Breen's son Patrick Breen* (p. 109).
49. Three members of the Royal Artillery prior to sailing on the *Khedive Ismail.* Patrick Breen is on the right of the picture, *courtesy of the late Patrick Breen's son Patrick Breen* (p. 109).
50. Certificate sent to Mrs Eva Henbest, *courtesy of Maureen Macaire* (p. 110).
51. Ordinary Telegraphist Roy Henbest, RN, *courtesy of Maureen Macaire* (p. 110).
52. Maureen Macaire, Tom Fox and the author on 13th February 1994, after the Wrens' Memorial Service in London, *author's collection* (p. 111).
53. The memorial to all the Women's Transport/Territorial Service who were killed in the 2nd World War. It is set on the north wall of St Paul's Church, Wilton Place, Knightsbridge and was unveiled in 1948, *author's collection* (p. 111).

BIBLIOGRAPHY AND UNPUBLISHED SOURCES

Ballard, Robert D., *The Discovery of the Titanic* (London: Hodder & Stoughton/Madison Press, 1987).

British Vessels Lost at Sea 1939–1945 (London: HMSO, 1947).

Carpenter, Dorr and Polmar, Norman, *Submarines of the Imperial Japanese Navy 1904–1945* (Annapolis, United States: National Institute Press, 1986).

Chronicle of the Second World War (Essex: Longman).

Churchill, Winston, *The Second World War*, Volume V: *Closing the Ring*, Appendix C, page 615.

Connell, Gordon G., *Fighting Destroyer* (London: William Kimber, 1976).

Grossmith, Frederick, *The Sinking of the Laconia. A Tragedy in the Battle of the Atlantic* (Stamford: Paul Watkins, 1995).

Keegan, John, *Encyclopedia of World War II* (London: Hamlyn, 1977).

Lloyd's War Losses. The Second World War. Volume 1. British Allied and Neutral Merchant Vessels sunk or damaged by war causes (London: Lloyds of London Press, 1989).

Rowher, Jürgen, *Axis Submarine Successes 1939–1945* (Annapolis, United States: Naval Institute Press, 1983).

Young, John M., *Britain's Sea War. A Diary of Ship Losses 1939–1945* (London: Stephens, 1975).

REGISTERS ISSUED BY THE IMPERIAL
WAR GRAVES COMMISSION

The BOMBAY MEMORIAL, Memorial Register 15, Parts 1 to 4, 1939–1945.

The BROOKWOOD MEMORIAL, Memorial Register 36, 1939–1945.

The CHATHAM MEMORIAL, Memorial Register 1, Parts 1 to 7, 1939–1945.

The EAST AFRICAN MEMORIAL, Memorial Register 18, Parts 1 and 2, 1939–1945.

The LEE-ON-SOLENT MEMORIAL, Memorial Register 5, 1939–1945.

The LIVERPOOL MEMORIAL, Memorial Register 4, 1939–1945.

The LOWESTOFT MEMORIAL, Memorial Register 6, 1939–1945.

The MERCHANT NAVY MEMORIAL, Tower Hill, London, Memorial Register 22, 1939–1945.

The PLYMOUTH MEMORIAL, Memorial Register 2, Parts 1 to 10, 1939–1945.

The PORTSMOUTH MEMORIAL, Memorial Register 3, Parts 1 to 10, 1939–1945.

BIBLIOGRAPHY

PUBLIC RECORDS OFFICE

ADM2/90 Dictionaries of Disasters at Sea during the age 1824 – 1962 (Volumes 1 & 2).

ADM53/119538 HMS *Hawkins* – log 5th –17th February 1944.

ADM199/157 Report on the loss of the SS *Mohamed Ali El-Kebir*.

ADM199/526 Convoy KR8, including Board of Enquiry held on 16th and 17th February 1944 specifically dealing with the circumstances attending the loss of the Troopship SS *Khedive Ismail* on 12th February 1944. Pages 43/43A, 45 to 82, 85, 89 to 128, 134A to 143, 145 to 148, 152 to 154.

ADM199/682 CM convoys (and others).

ADM199/1025 African Convoys September to early December 1943.

ADM199/1035 Convoys KR5, KR6 and KR7 (and others).

ADM199/2052 U-boat incident report – 13th February 1944.

ADM199/2061 U-boat incident reports (various monthly updates on the observations of the war against enemy submarines, including reports on new weaponry being developed and tested).

ADM199/2133 Report by Chief Officer L.C. Hill, concerning the sinking of the troopship *Mohamed Ali El-Kebir*.

ADM199/2147 Report by 2nd Officer, Mr C.H.R. Munday, concerning the sinking of the troopship SS *Khedive Ismail.*

ADM199/2289 War Diary – Most Secret. 13 messages sent 12th to 21st February 1944.

GUILDHALL LIBRARY

Confidential Movements of Vessels on Special Government Service 1939–44.

Confidential Shipping Movements: January 1940 – March 1944.

Lloyd's Voyage Record Cards *Aconcagua/Khedive Ismail* 1927–44.

Lloyd's Voyage Record Cards *Teno/Mohamed Al El Kebir* 1927–40.

Lloyd's Confidential Sheets: January – December 1943.

Lloyd's List and Shipping Gazettes: January 1941 – February 1944.

Lloyd's Weekly Casualty Reports: January/February 1926.

Lloyd's Weekly Casualty Reports: July/September/October 1928.

Lloyd's Weekly Casualty Reports: October – December 1934.

ROYAL ARTILLERY HISTORICAL TRUST

Royal Artillery Commemoration Book 1939–45, pages 347–350.

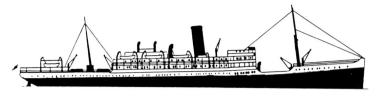

INDEX

Note: the index attempts to cover the main text of the book comprehensively but it does not cover the alphabetical lists of names in the appendices. The compiler was the author.